SAINTS IN LOVE

Saints in Love

The Forgotten Loves Between Holy Women and Men and How They Can Make Our Relationships Divine

CAROLE HALLUNDBAEK

With the poetry of

POPE JOHN PAUL II

A Crossroad Book
The Crossroad Publishing Company
New York

The Crossroad Publishing Company
16 Penn Plaza, Suite 1550, New York, NY 10001

Printed in the United States of America
Library of Congress Cataloging-in-Publication Data

Hallundbaek, Carole, 1963-
  Saints in love : the forgotten loves between men and women saints and how they help
us build relationships today : Clare and Francis of Assisi, Teresa of Avila and John of
the Cross, Catherine of Siena and Pope Gregory XI, Francis de Sales & Jane de
Chantal, with the poetry of Pope John Paul II /Carole Hallundbaek.
     p. cm.
  Includes bibliographical references.
  ISBN-13: 978-0-8245-2445-6 (alk. paper)
  ISBN-10: 0-8245-2445-4 (alk. paper)
  1. Monastic and religious life. 2. Celibacy—Catholic Church. 3.
Love—Religious aspects—Catholic Church. 4. Friendship—Religious
aspects—Catholic Church. 5. Man-woman relationships—Religious
aspects—Catholic Church. I. Title.

BX2440.H35 2007
282.092'2—dc22
[B]

2007021987

1 2 3 4 5 6 7 8 9   14 13 12 11 10 09 08 07

Contents

DEDICATION

To my husband, Michael

And to the memory of Pope John Paul II
when he was a young poet
named Karol

Divine Love: A Way In

Years ago, the man who would become my husband looked at me one day and said, "Your love for me helps me to believe in God's love for me." The connection that he made – perceiving the divine love in our very human love – touched me deeply. It was what I had hoped and searched for, and once it was uttered, I felt all my years of searching had come to a close. The connection one man made seemed like a miracle – yet it was also a simple and basic revelation: God's love for us becomes real through our experiences of human love.

The divine love is something we recognize deep down as our origin and our destiny; we seek it, and believe it is available to us, at this moment, in all our relationships. Chances are we already possess this glimpse of heaven in our relationship, even if we are unable to recognize it among all the busyness, work, family responsibilities, and financial commitments.

"Human loves can be glorious images of Divine love," wrote C. S. Lewis. But what does the inspired relationship look like?

The inspired couple? The inspired marriage? The inspired parents, teachers, friends, employers? The image of that divine love – and the path to helping it manifest and sustain in our own lives – can elude even the most spiritually receptive or religious souls.

The saints embody the unity of divine love and human form, yet we often find it difficult to see how the spiritual journeys of the saints connect with our own. As a younger person, I looked at images of St. Francis of Assisi and saw the peaceful man alone with nature, caressing a deer while a bird rested on his shoulder. I felt glad for these artistic renderings of his inner peace, but I did not know the nuts and bolts of how he arrived at it.

It was not until I discovered, when I was about eighteen years old, that there was an eighteen-year-old girl whom Francis loved, dedicated himself to, and risked the Franciscan brotherhood for, that I began to find a way into the journey of the beloved saint. It was not his distant divinity that taught me; it was his passionate humanity: his love for Clare, his flesh-and-blood struggles with co-workers and finances, his personal challenges with family members, his joys and evolving talents, his search for his place in the world – the many ways in which his life was like mine – and possibly yours. This was a saint I could take hold of! I had found a way in.

Inspired, I began to unearth the larger relationship of Francis and Clare, and, later, relationships between other sainted men and women in history whose great capacities for human love act as guides for our own relationships today. The very real-life experiences shared by these "couples" helped me tremendously in my own life and as I helped others as a spiritual director. Each of these saints had a special someone who helped to inspire, guide, and form them. I have distilled their stories here as a helpful guide pertinent to our relationships today.

~❧

This book first began while I was working toward a graduate degree in theology and religion in the mid-1990s at Fordham, New York's Jesuit university. I was a Roman Catholic student steeped in the Roman Catholic tradition. It was a time when Pope John Paul II invoked the term "infallible" about the church's position on the possibility (or impossibility) of women's ordination to the priesthood. Many students, professors, and religious alike responded in the classroom with feelings of disappointment, deep sadness, or indignation. From their pain, some female students challenged the older male professors angrily and confronted the young men on the ordination track. The professors tried to comfort, the younger men stood speechless, perhaps due to immaturity, or perhaps the shock of confrontation. I watched relationships change and become strained, and that was the most difficult thing for me, after such a close-knit time of study and growth together as a theological community. Outside the classroom, we began to see American Catholics and Episcopalians trade places: conservative Anglican priests who disapproved of the ordination of women in their denomination were received into the Catholic church, even with their wives and children; progressive Catholic priests left to become Episcopal, and the same migrations were happening in the pews among parishioners – all stemming from the basic relationship between man and woman and God, a relationship that is at its core not political but sacramental.

And so I began to write, to address these issues concerning relationship and community. I did so primarily as a gift to the church during a difficult time of pain and challenge around evolving gender roles and other emerging stumbling blocks in the church's relationships among colleagues. Eventually a book began to form, rooted in tradition yet dedicated to love, imagination, and growth together as a community – toward a refreshed vision of ourselves, our interactions, and our future.

Since then, my own life has evolved to encompass marriage, children, and years of work as an author and facilitator in the field of ecumenical faith, spiritual direction, and counseling. I came to realize that these saints and their relationships are helpful not only to the institutional church but also to all of my personal interactions. Surprisingly, these relationships often shed light on marriage, work, family, healthy attachments, emotional healing, and more.

Along the way, I discovered beautiful poetry written by Pope John Paul II when he was a young man yet unburdened by the pressures of office. Passionate, even romantic, deeply intuitive and visionary, his work speaks to the beauty and dignity of the experience of men and women and is included here to accompany the saints' journeys. I hope you enjoy it. Published under his given name, I feel these poems by the young Karol capture the essence of each pairing, their time, their deepest concern, and their relationship.

As we journey together through this book, we will enter the enduring and transformative bonds of the profound partnerships of Clare and Francis of Assisi; Teresa of Avila and John of the Cross; Catherine of Siena and Pope Gregory XI; and Francis de Sales and Jane de Chantal. We will do so in light of particular facets of their passionate friendships – love, sexuality, work, spiritual growth, humor, societal roles, challenges, strengths, and their mutual inspiration. In each case, their experience holds for us something galvanizing and unique to apply to our own relationships.

Even though the stories of these men and women and their life-giving relationships have been told before, I want to share with you my insights into some specific events and experiences along their journeys. These pivotal events reconnected Francis and Clare, Teresa and John, Catherine and Gregory, and Francis de Sales and Jane to the divine love within, removing internal obstacles, unveiling each saint's authentic self, and establishing his or her true role in life and among humanity. These key moments and interactions changed the course of their lives forever. Their discoveries offer valuable lessons for our relationships today – at home, at work, in community, and with God.

On my bed when I think of you,
I muse on you in the watches of the night,
for you have always been my help;

in the shadows of your wings I rejoice;
my heart clings to you,
your right hand supports me.

—Psalm 63, New Jerusalem Bible

There is an African tradition of love songs so pure, the listener cannot tell if the singer is singing of a lover or of God. In our own tradition of popular music, Simon & Garfunkel's "Bridge Over Troubled Water" would be among them, the loving singer pledging to "dry all the tears" of the beloved, as God promises in the New Testament. Peter Gabriel's "In Your Eyes" would be among them, the singer considering the lover's eyes as a doorway to a thousand churches. The Bee Gees' "How Deep Is Your Love" praises the lover as a savior and a light in the darkness. Songs like these bring together and celebrate the categories of divine love and human love. They are also perennial favorites – and perhaps that should not be of great surprise. These are melodies that haunt the soul; lyrics that I would sing to my husband or to my children to comfort them; words I would hope the angels would wrap around my own heart in my hour of need. Music has this ability, to create a sacred bridge between our worldly hands and our most exalted visions, combining math and sound in a way that penetrates the whole of our brain, subduing any division. At its truest, music is both human and divine. We cannot resist.

Similarly, Christology teaches us that the person of Jesus is fully human and fully divine. Of course he is; he is Love. True Love is fully human and fully divine. It creates, it heals, it forgives, it sustains, it illumines, and it carries hope. It is the bridge to peace. It is peace, uniting heaven and earth. And like God's grace, it is freely given to us, a blessing we can help make manifest here and now.

This love is no different from the love in your marriage, or for your children, your friends, or your colleagues. What may feel different in your life is how you spend your time. There is an adage, "He travels fastest who travels alone," and it may give the impression that fullness of spirituality is attainable by monks, priests, brothers and sisters, or retreatants – that is, those who appear to be single or unattached – and not for those with a family to raise and never enough solitude or time. But the answer does not lie in time.

Your life is holy, and your love is holy. Your breakfast rush, your kids on their way to school, your daily commute, your eyes made tired by the PC, your wondering about what dinner to make, your wondering about which bills to pay, your perpetual pile of waiting laundry – all holy.

There are so many facets to the jewel of relationship, so many opportunities for connection, and so many missed. There is so much love, and so many ways to share it, lose it, and find it once more on this earth. We know how important relationships are, in all their manifestations. We recognize that they are a barometer of sorts of our spiritual and emotional development: the sense of growth and peace that shines within us when we have truly forgiven a past hurt and we rekindle a friendship; the loss or regret that we may feel when we know we have not faced up to a conflict or challenge. All our interactions can be sources of peace, joy, or grief as our life progresses.

At one time or another, we are all called upon to grow in relationship, to surrender to new life that may not be on familiar emotional ground. Our response to that call, whether trusting or fearful, can liberate us to a greater adventure of love, or may limit our fullness of experience to the maze of our habitual thinking, the ways we have always thought of love, relationship, ourselves, and our age-old reactions when presented with the possibility of commitment, or intimacy, or even our dreams-come-true. Perhaps that maze is a safe and familiar place. But does it bring peace and joy?

Many of the saints also were called to move beyond their mode of habitual thinking and behavior. In this book, we will explore the specific crossroads at which they allowed themselves to change their thinking, or clear away whatever surrounded their heart that kept them separated from the ultimate love of God and humanity.

Clare and Francis of Assisi were mystics, contemplatives, and spiritual spouses devoted to God and poverty of spirit. Affectionately nick-named Brother Sun and Sister Moon because of references in Francis's prayers, this man and woman launched the Franciscan orders in the thirteenth century, possibly the greatest movement in Christian history. Their unique love for each other, their transcendent vision of God and humanity, and their understanding of the transformation of daily life continue to delight and inspire us today. While many have tried to marginalize Clare in his life, Francis said, "Don't believe that I do not love her with a perfect love." From their relationship, we learn about courage, risk, intimacy, and keeping our love relationship vibrant and life-giving.

Teresa of Avila and John of the Cross were sixteenth-century Spanish mystics, both doctors of the church, and both gifted and inspired writers. Teresa, a humorous, fiery woman, gave young John a job and together they reformed their order, founding the Discalced Carmelites. This great task was lived out in the work-place, and so we will explore their relationship lived out as colleagues in a corporate atmosphere. In this regard, the most important lesson Teresa, in particular, needed to learn was one of honesty in relationship, healthy attachments, and true freedom to love. Additionally, their mystical writings (notably her Interior Castle and his heady poetry of spiritual union with God) are complementary voices that raise up the male and female essences of God and humanity in the most passionate embrace of beautiful language.

Though many spiritual luminaries could be the patron saint of Italy, the country's spiritual guardian is not Francis, Anthony, or

Thomas Aquinas, but Catherine of Siena. A fourteenth-century theologian and doctor of the church, Catherine lived during the time of the Avignon popes when the seat of the Church was moved to France during a period of tremendous political strife in Italy. Pope Gregory XI invited her wise counsel, and their friendship paved the way for his return to Rome. From Catherine and Gregory we learn of an adult image of God, mature spirituality, honoring our conscience, and living as our authentic selves in community.

Francis de Sales was the passionate preacher who swayed people's hearts with the phrase "Live Jesus!" as opposed to "Long Live the King." Jane de Chantal was a wealthy widow who turned to Francis for spiritual direction. They stood on the brink of modernity, about the year 1600, and co-founded over eighty Houses of the Visitation across France for the purpose of bringing out the sacred in the people's everyday lives.

Even more moving were their personal letters of spiritual direction, letters that are on fire with their love for God, their love for each other as human beings, and their devotion to each other's journey – and to ours. It may be said that Francis and Jane were able to express in writing what Clare and Francis of Assisi were able to share only in poignant silence. Francis and Jane held nothing back. Their communication is so very important for our spiritual life, the daily life of our relationships, and the growth and health of community. From them we learn the ultimate spiritual freedom of mutuality, and how we all guide and shape each other along our life's journey toward self-actualization and fulfillment.

Francis and Clare, Teresa and John, Catherine and Gregory, Francis and Jane – these men and women soared together, and their love for each other infused Christianity with growth and vitality – Franciscan, Carmelite, and Salesian spirituality – giving new life and breath to the experience of faith worldwide. Perhaps this should come as no surprise – such are the creative forces when masculine and feminine unite.

Now let us journey into the past to recall how human love helped lead the saints to divine love. Let us learn how their love can illumine our own.

❖

Feet search the grass. The earth. Insects
drill the scenery, swaying the stream of the sun.
Feet wear down cobbles, the cobbled street
wears down feet. No pathos. Thoughts in the crowd
unspoken.

Take a thought, if you can – plant its root
in the artisan's hands, in the fingers
of women typing eight hours a day;
black letters hang from reddened eyelids.

Take a thought, make man complete,
or allow him to begin himself anew,
or let him just help You perhaps
and you lead him on.

Why is it not so, Magdalene, Simon of Cyrene?
Do you remember that first step which you are still
taking all the time?

—KAROL WOJTYLA, 1958

A Wedding of Souls

CLARE AND FRANCIS OF ASSISI

Benvenuto — welcome!

It seems to rise from the rich brown Umbrian earth, as though lifted high on the upraised olive branches of the orchards beneath it: Assisi. You don't need a map to find this ancient walled city not far from Rome, even if arriving by car in the dead of night. Your heart brings you there. The road turns a bit, and suddenly, there's Assisi – a medieval beacon, a city of hearts on a hill, hearts made natural by God's love.

Your tired feet find their way into town through the *porta*, the gate, beside the basilica. You're quietly welcomed by your hosts wherever you're staying, given a good hot meal – and perhaps even a souvenir – before your head finally surrenders into the deep down of your awaiting pillow.

The black night guarded by Sister Moon is stark and silent – more silent than expected for this famous place of pilgrimage – except if it begins to rain. Then thunder rolls along the hills surrounding you in this valley, its haunting sound gathering momen-tum and volume until you find yourself staring wide-eyed at the dark from your little bed, wondering if it was true, what they told you as a child, about thunder being angels tap dancing.

The dawn arrives gently as Brother Sun coaxes you from your bed to peek from your balcony at the dark, fishscale rooftops, the wet cobblestones, the misty morning hills. The scents of hearty bread and heartier coffee waft into your awakening senses. Downstairs on the red-tiled patio, a butterfly or bumblebee is an unexpected breakfast guest. But you don't mind, as you consider the velvety texture and crimson coloring of the potted impatiens beside your table. A gentle breeze lifts your hair, and your heart, and always – always – the birds fly above Assisi.

It has been more than eight hundred years since the Poor Man and Poor Ladies of Assisi followed their calling into love and into his-tory. Yet one's senses are deliciously heightened when in this place. If you desire, you may carry the lay of the land in your arms, close to your heart; feel the imprint of the sunlight on your eye-lids; look intently for the first time at the winding bones of an olive tree. All shared meals feel blessed. Red wine tastes better, richer – perhaps, you think, because the Umbrian vines that pro-duced this year's vintage link us somehow to the grapes Francis reaped all those centuries ago! Oh, yes, Assisi does bring out the romance, the spiritual ardor in us with its closeness to Christ's table and to heaven.

But Francis did more than plant grapevines at San Damiano – he planted a seed of love for humanity, planted it deep down in the Spoleto soil that nurtures the seed to bring forth a perennial harvest. Every year thousands travel from around the world to visit Assisi and walk where Francis and Clare walked. Perhaps they don't remember where or when they first heard of St. Francis and St. Clare, but once they heard the saints' story, it became part of their spiritual fabric forever.

Though they are among the most beloved saints in Christian history and the events of their lives are among the most moving, it is difficult to tell the story of Francis, Clare, and the blossoming of the Franciscan orders. Because they heal our hearts, inspire us, and fill us with hope, they have spawned much legend. Their stories occasionally are associated with certain miracles and visions that may have in fact occurred, or that may reflect the deepest desires and wishes of our own hearts. Who could blame us? Francis and Clare embodied for each other and for us the real possibility of living the ideal gospel life.

Conversely, as often occurs in the church, there were those who were made ill-at-ease by the great partnership of Francis and Clare – disturbed by their complementary genders, his charisma, the young woman's beauty – and they have attempted to marginalize Clare in biographies of Francis, making her almost superfluous to his vocation. We in the church still struggle to allow a religious man, even in memory, to be affected by a woman, to allow her to be vital to his mission, to allow him to care enough to invest personally in her journey, recognizing it as part of his own.

Yet Francis dared to resemble Christ in this way too. Once, pressed by a throng of followers clutching at him, Jesus discerned the touch of one woman. "Who touched me?" Jesus asked, which must have seemed a ludicrous question in the moment. A hundred hands were touching him. But when the woman who needed heal-ing reached out in her humility and utter faith, she *touched* Jesus, penetrating his consciousness. They connected silently, two souls in a barrage of activity and excitement.

I believe this is what the *Povorello*, the Little Poor Man, expe-rienced with the Lady Clare, this radiant light who would embody for him the fulfillment of his own vision. Francis saw what Clare would become, even before she did, and encouraged and nurtured her passion so that she could fulfill her destiny even as he met his own.

What else can this be called but love?

Footsteps: Assisi

It was late summer when I visited Assisi, finally arriving at the place I had longed to see for years: San Damiano – the church that Francis rebuilt and that later became the convent of Clare.

I stood at the top of a cobblestone road that led rather steeply down to the site. The stones were exceedingly smooth, as though worn fine over the centuries by the pilgrimages of many souls. And I was wearing new sandals, strappy little leather sandals, Italian, with shiny smooth soles. There was virtually no friction between my shoes and the steep path, and so I baby-stepped a lit-

tle down the slippery stones, sliding here, and again, and once
more. It was a terribly difficult approach to my journey's end, and
one that had taken me completely by surprise.

I tried various moves such as walking down sideways apiece,
and I found myself wishing for sneakers or hiking boots or any
other "sole-ful" option back at the hotel. Frustrated, I finally
asked an unseen authority how on earth people walked here. The
answer came as softly as the September breeze, an answer that
would remind me that I needed to bring no firmer grasp or special
preparation or tools to my spiritual journey. *Take off your sandals.*
I needed to bring nothing but my own unfettered self.

I removed my shoes, stored them in my tote, and stepped onto
the stones with bare feet. The stones were warm. Soft. And welcoming. Walking from then on was simple and silent, an immediate connection to the humility and love that walked there long
before me. But Francis had learned this too: Christianity is a cobblestone religion best lived out on foot.

Beginnings

He was born to the Bernadone family in Assisi around 1182, the son of a French woman and a respectable if stern father who made his living as a cloth merchant. His mother, Pica, had him baptized Giovanni, or John, after John the Baptist. In a typical marital spat for which this couple would be known, his father, Pietro, insisted on renaming him Francesco, or Frenchman. Regardless of the change of given name, the child would grow to be true to the essence of his baptismal name, becoming a herald and bridge for a great spiritual transition.

She was born Chiara di Favorone in Assisi about 12 years later, to a powerful and wealthy noble family of Lombardi descent. It is said that her mother, Ortolana, while praying during her pregnancy, heard the reassuring words, "Fear not, for you will safely give birth to a clear light that will shine on all the earth." And so the baby was named Chiara, or clear shining one. Spiritual and compassionate by nature, the child Clare would give her meals to the poor and was known for her humility and generosity.

The two children were raised within the medieval walls of this ancient city. They were baptized in the same font in the same church, the Cathedral of San Rufino. Francis and Clare grew up speaking their dialect of Italian, but they knew Latin and probably spoke French as well. Later, this man and this woman would break out from the spiritual womb of these medieval walls and together yield one of the greatest movements in Christian history – the Franciscan orders – but not without the divine love's demand of courage, vulnerability, and great risk to them both.

THE MAN

He was a most eloquent man, a man of cheerful countenance, of kindly aspect; he was immune to cowardice, free of insolence.

He was of medium height, closer to shortness; his head was moderate in size and round, his face a bit long and prominent, his forehead smooth and low; his

eyes were moderate size, black and round; his hair was black, his eyebrows straight, his nose symmetrical, thin and straight; his ears were upright but small; his temples smooth.

His speech was peaceable, fiery and sharp; his voice was strong, sweet and sonorous.

His neck was slender; his shoulders straight; his arms short; his hands slender; his fingers long; his nails extended; his legs were thin; his feet small. His skin was delicate; his flesh very spare. He wore rough garments. He slept but very briefly. He gave most generously.

—THOMAS OF CELANO, *The Life of St. Francis*

THE WOMAN

She was the first flower in Francis' garden, and she shone like a radiant star, fragrant as a flower blossoming white and pure in springtime.

—ST. BONAVENTURE

Her face was oval, her forehead spacious, her color dazzling, and her eyebrows and hair very fair. A celestial smile played in her eyes and around her mouth, her nose was well fashioned and slightly aquiline. . .

She was noble by birth, but still more noble by grace, and she was of angelic purity. Though still young, she was mature before her time, fervent in the service of God, endowed with rare prudence and deepest humility, she was one of those great souls whom the human tongue cannot worthily praise.

—THOMAS OF CELANO, *The Life of St. Clare*

A World Like Ours

Although Francis and Clare lived during the medieval period in Italy, they experienced many of the same challenges we face today. While they did not have the presence (or omnipresence) of electronic media and communication, they did grow up with the seemingly perpetual issues of war and conflict, both away and at home; the social, physical, and deeply spiritual struggle of those who have and those who have not; and the expectations of family and society. Money was important. Status was important. Appearance was important. Clothes were important. Finally, at the center of their town, and the storm of typical teen pressures, was the grand and stalwart footing of Mother Church – and a way of living that would one day leave Francis feeling hollow, inspiring his search for new meaning.

Youth is a time of great quests of all kinds, and particularly between the ages of seventeen and twenty-two. It is a time of searching, when we stretch our boundaries, push envelopes, experiment, and learn who we are in relation to the world around us. It is also a deeply symbolic period of engagement between our emerging self and our origin – God. We feel the exciting onset and power of creation, freedom, faith, and life's adventure. Everything takes on enormous meaning: the grades we seek, the sports we play, the dreams we have, the colors we wear, the music we love, the friends we collect, the hobbies we enjoy, even the way we practice signing our name – all these things seem to identify us, at least for a time.

This is also a peak period of spiritual questing, when young people initiate their adult faith journey by questioning their belief systems as well as those of their parents and others in authority. It is no coincidence that many who enter the religious life do so at this age. Clare was eighteen when she answered her call, and Francis in his early twenties. It is a time of inner sculpting, of taking the experiences and icons of one's childhood, and shaping them into the stepping-stones of adult spirituality, paving the first pathway on which we will stand as we leave our childhood and enter society.

CHIVALRY

Also at this time in history, the very real and symbolic image of chivalry ran deeply in the consciousness of both Clare and Francis. Clare had seven knights in her family, and Francis was becoming known for his own exploits as a warrior. As he grew,

Francis came to have the same dreams of knighthood and battle as any other young man – dreams of glory and riches and conquest of men and women. It was this life to which he aspired for many years. Thomas of Celano, the first official biographer of Francis and Clare, would write that it was in this manner that Francis literally "wasted the first twenty-five years of his life." However, the dreams and goals of chivalry would not leave Francis and Clare in their lifetime. Instead, something would happen that would lead them to redefine chivalry – to transform its image of riches and the lady for whom one dares to give all.

The knight would no longer be on horseback, in armor, a powerful and armed conqueror; he would stand on the earth, unshod, poor, the embodiment of compassion. The lady would no longer be the privileged princess, representing wealth and earthly beauty, but would become Lady Poverty – the song of one's soul, unadorned, and the embodiment of love, service, and mercy.

THE STRANGER

Our conversion begins, said Clare, when we begin . . . the process of turning our eyes from ourselves unto God. There are blocks between ourselves and God which must be cleared if we are to have an uninterrupted view. There is an inner maze, our personal labyrinth, whose dark ways must be flooded with the light of Christ.

—SR. FRANCES TERESA, OSC, *This Living Mirror: Reflections on Clare of Assisi*

After a childhood lived in the sunlight of freedom and comfort, Francis found himself within very "dark ways" – the confines of prison. As a young warrior in his early twenties, Francis and his fellow knights from Assisi lost a battle against Perugia, a nearby city. They were taken prisoner, most likely for ransom, and Francis was held for about a year. Although he tried to bolster the morale of his friends with good spirit and humor, prison would take its toll.

Francis fell terribly ill during this time of captivity. Though difficult, prison can be a fertile ground for conversion – and it set the stage for change in Francis. The English mystic Julian of Norwich said, "Your cell will teach you everything," and during that year, imprisonment acted as a precursor to the monastic experience for Francis. Within those walls, Francis saw how his peers' worldly illusions, familiar roles and desires, and even their personal characteristics were drained, leaving them alone, perhaps for the first time, with their life's inner emptiness. As a prisoner of war, he saw how his very best dreams, intentions, and actions had led only here – to isolation, loss, sickness, and pain.

Francis was eventually released by his captors, perhaps out of pity or perhaps because of his illness: he simply would no longer command a ransom as a hostage. Sick, solitary, and probably in shock, he made his way back to Assisi. Although his family nursed him back to physical health, his spiritual health would require another doctor, a Divine Physician, over the coming months.

There followed a time of uncertainty for Francis, typical perhaps for a young man; it was a time of "finding himself." He had come home, but he felt displaced somehow. He had returned to work for his father, but he was distracted. He appeared restless, brooding. He seemed to have occasional "spells" of introverted behavior – times in which he seemed to his friends to be "somewhere else," gazing into space, unreachable – so unlike the old Francis. In fact, when he was like this, his friends thought it was because of a woman. They thought that Francis had fallen in love and was walking around in a smitten haze. And perhaps, in a way, he had. But the divine love that was working in him was God communicating in ways Francis would not understand for some time – in dreams, in mystical visions, through creation, and through people.

TOUCHING THE UNTOUCHABLE

"Love don't make things nice. It ruins everything. It breaks your heart.
It makes things a mess. We're not here to make things perfect.
We are here to ruin ourselves, and to break our hearts, and
love the wrong people . . . and die."
    —A philosophy of love, from the 1987 film Moonstruck

Following his time in prison, there would come an exchange with someone that would be the most transformational event of Francis's life to that point: the leper. In Francis's time, people suffering from the terrible disease of leprosy were set apart, literally, from other people. Yet, in Assisi, lepers were hired for hard manual labor, even by Francis's father. Leprosy is contagious, and many of those afflicted wore bells that would ring as they walked to let others know they were close by or approaching. Francis, like anyone else, feared proximity with lepers and was frightened and repulsed by their appearance.

One day Francis went for a ride on his horse in the great fields around Assisi. At some point along his journey, a leper stepped out into the road. Francis stopped suddenly. At first he reacted as he always had: he was shocked, frightened, and nauseated at the sight of the man's crumbling flesh. He turned his horse around – his instinct was to bolt – and for a split second his legs tightened in fear and he began to dig his heels into his horse's side. But something stopped him, something like a gentle hand on his shoulder. Something invited him to respond differently this time. People ran away from Jesus, too, ran from the one whose flesh was crucified.... Francis did not bolt. He turned to face the leper again.

Francis climbed down slowly from his horse and walked gently to the man. In an action that must have startled them both, he took hold of the leper's hand, and he kissed it. He learned to love "the wrong person." He would no longer fear the crucified flesh but would befriend it now at all cost, seeing God in the most afflicted, alienated, and powerless person. Francis surrendered his ultimate fear, and somehow it made him stronger, even physically, to serve among the lepers. And perhaps the leper surrendered his fear too, releasing the pain of alienation that he would no longer need to hide from Francis. Both recalled, with broken hearts and bleeding flesh, that they were innocent children of God. On a silent dusty road among sunlit fields, Francis made the leper his brother.

It was over. It was over, and it had begun. Francis saw the miracle of life. He saw the miracle of everything. Earth. Innocence. Love. Beauty. Now there would be no return to the old ways, the old values, or old prizes. He was free – free to love as Christ did. And any change toward Christ brings challenge.

Alienation was new to the popular Francis; his radical openness to all, including lepers, alienated him from even those closest to him. The admired and charming son of the affluent cloth merchant began to wear tatters and wander in the streets of Assisi, begging. He had become a stranger to those who thought they knew him so well.

FAMILY

He was looked upon as a fool by many, and as he passed by he was driven away with stones and foul abuse, both by his relatives and by others, all of which ill-treatment and contumely he bore patiently, as though he were deaf and dumb.

—from *The Little Flowers of St. Francis,* IV

The divine love would permeate Francis's heart, and it would transform all his relationships, with the earth, the church, men, women, and his family. For Francis, saying goodbye to his former way of life would include saying goodbye to his parents – if not forever, then for the time being throughout this time of transition. His father was unable to accept the changes occurring in Francis, and so in some way had already rejected Francis's new and strange perceptions and desires for another way of life.

Relationships come down to family. One way or the other, whether we accept this or deny it, our life and our meaning come down to our family of origin; the family and loving bonds we create of our own commitment as adults; and our place as brothers and sisters among the human family.

The word "family" can conjure up completely different images for people – much the same way as the word "God" or "church" – based on our own personal experiences and where we might be at any given time along our inner journey. These are powerful words and concepts, inextricably connected in our minds, memories, and emotions: Family ➤ God ➤ Church.

Presently, two cinematic icons in our popular culture – Harry Potter and Willy Wonka – provide the current generation two distinct responses to family challenges: Harry, whose parents have died, misses and searches for them, and therefore seeks inner peace and identity; and the runaway Wonka, who denies his very-much-alive father, creates his own world within a world, and humorously gags on the word "parents" and other natural longings.

As children, our experience of parents influences our image and understanding of God, and later church or belief as a whole. For many, this is a natural flow of thought and comfort. For others, "God" and "church" simply have nothing to do with each other. Perhaps most moving, I have seen many faithful people struggle painfully with the churches, bringing familial hopes and expectations to their clergy or community, and ultimately rejecting the community with feelings of utter disappointment and isolation. Perceiving the church, and clergy, as a failing parental figure, they throw the baby Jesus out with the bathwater.

THERE WOULD COME A DAY

At last, there would come a day when Francis could no longer live this in-between life, living between the death of his old life and his yet unknown new life. A choice had to be made. Frustrated and confused, his own father brought his son's "condition," as it was called, before the bishop in the square of the cathedral where Francis was baptized. This marked the return to a beginning place for Francis, the place of christening – but this time he came not with the innocence of a child but now with the renewed innocence of adulthood, the innocence of rediscovering what is precious because of what has been lost, and what has been found once more. He had lost his illusions of worldly glory, lost his friends, and lost his reputation. What he found again was his original connection to the divine.

The entire issue of Francis's change created a confrontation between the will of his father on earth and his Father in heaven. In the end, Francis made his choice. He stood in the public square before the townspeople and clergy and, in a moment both painful and freeing, returned his possessions, all the clothes he was wearing, even his name to his father. The divine love broke the bonds of childhood – and Francis would walk away from Assisi a new Adam, free to face his open future.

God's call to Francis was also a call to his parents. Francis's mother and father, the most important relations in his life to that point, would need to learn to reimagine their son, and the roles and meaning of family, if they were to continue in relationship. If they did not answer God's call to grow, they would live a kind of half-life as parents, cut off in their grief. Sadly, they were not able to support Francis on his journey.

The family is a system, its different members working together somehow, finding a way to live – in health, enjoyment, struggle, or suffering. When one of the members finds it necessary to go a different way, it presents a jolt to the entire system, like a wrench in the gears. The other members are also thrown off kilter. Like Francis, the one who decides to take a different path may be looked upon as a traitor. Many who have answered the call to religious life have experienced this; also, many of those who have gone through the life-death-rebirth journey of divorce and remarriage; and others in the process of 12-Step recovery. One motion toward new life can send shockwaves of change throughout our relations, like ripples across the face of a pond.

The family is a storyteller, carrying on the "myth of genera-tions." Some sons and daughters write new stories that may or may not reflect the well-worn tradition or myth of the family. Can the family incorporate their new stories, celebrating their part of the myth? Or must a new book begin?

When we pray together, is there one way to pray, bonding the family with the strong mortar of familiar words? Or is there also room to pray differently, with changing voices and words, invit-ing the Spirit to breathe over our thoughts and meals and rituals?

For Francis, the answer might be no; for Clare, the family sit-uation would be different. Her relationship with her family would continue throughout her life, as we will see later. In either case, whether supported or not by blood relations, God would be there for Francis and Clare, lighting their way with love.

BROTHER SUN

I met in the street a very poor young man who was in love.
His hat was old, his coat worn, his cloak was out at the elbows,
the water passed through his shoes - and the stars through his soul.

— VICTOR HUGO

His new life came to Francis like springtime – naturally and gen-tly, as it does when we fall in love with a person, with one's self, with life – at once as old as creation, and as instantaneous. How shining he was, like a newborn blade of grass. It was time to emerge from his cocoon of odd nothingness into the butterfly of Spirit. And somehow, it was simpler and easier than one would think. It was a kind of sidestep into a world that was always there, waiting for him. Francis was always a good soul; now the God who was working within him would make a bolder request of his energies and – as with St. Paul – would not expunge his personality, but would take his intelligence, generosity, and passion and redirect these gifts and abilities for which he had been known in his youth. The former "king of revels" would become a celebrant of grace.

Francis walked beyond the fortified walls of Assisi and came upon the ruins of San Damiano, an ancient church that had always fascinated him. He surveyed the broken structure, walking among the fallen stones. Then it came like a gentle hand on his shoulder. Francis turned around to see the simple crucifix there – no triumphant Christus Rex – but the man, the poor Jesus, looking directly at him from the cross. And he heard a voice: "Repair my house, Francesco, which as you can see, is in ruins."

He looked about him. Indeed, the walls of this holy place were crumbling and lay in ruins. He began to rebuild this small church, stone by stone.

Had he taken the message too literally? Was it meant to be a more symbolic suggestion for his life's work? Or did Francis merely begin with what lay immediately before him, realizing that this painstaking labor of love would be a process whereby he might begin to anchor his soul, to be still, to focus his energy on building up rather than tearing down, as he had done as a warrior?

Francis succeeded in rebuilding that church, in which he lived during that time. He was able to use some of the old stones that lay in ruins and also required some new ones to replace those that were too weak or broken. And he became eager to restore other churches as well, next repairing the nearby church of St. Peter, and then a site that would become most precious of all to him: the Porziuncula, a tiny chapel about half a mile from Assisi in the mists of the Spoleto Valley.

With this simple life focused on restoration, Francis began to mature in his faith. Companions began to appear: Bernardo, a childhood friend, would be the first to join him in community. Others followed: Peter Cattani, Egidio, Filippo, Masseo, Rufino, Pacificus. They prayed. They worked. They helped the poor and infirm. They were drawn to simplicity and gratitude. In 1208, Francis discerned that they were meant to preach. They donned the cassock and cord for which the Franciscans are known to this day. In 1209, Pope Innocent III verbally approved of their form of life. Francis was twenty-seven.

SISTER MOON

She followed him because she loved the treasure. She heard him speak of what he had found, and a passage in her own heart opened up. They had found the same treasure in different caves, and they would share it with whomever they met in that sacred place below the surface of life. She was Clare and he was Francis, and together they would show the world its hidden heart.

—MURRAY BODO, OFM, *Clare: A Light in the Garden*

He knew, even as he rebuilt San Damiano. He knew who would be living there. He knew, as he carefully laid stone after stone, whose small feet would walk the narrow corridors, whose many teardrops shed for love of God would alight on the ground, whose prayers would yield rare blossoms like the roses in her balcony garden. And here he was, penniless, a spiritual husband, preparing the home he would give to her for her lifetime in love.

[Francis's] words inflamed the ardor of [Clare's] love and she longed to live the Gospel more intensively. His preaching . . . led her to seek a new way of living.

—*Acts of the Process of Canonization of Clare*, XVI, 3

Clare was becoming a young woman when she heard Francis preach in Assisi. Perhaps she had also witnessed the earlier scene at the cathedral when Francis faced his father before the bishop; her family home was adjacent to the cathedral. Francis's spiritual journey had been a stunningly public one, a journey bared before his neighbors, for better or worse. Hers was still private, a secret journey and hidden wish, lived out through dreams and acts of charity. Clare was beautiful, kind, and popular – and utterly alone. She required just one kindred soul.

Francis's spiritual vision evolved to embrace more than a dream shared with brothers; it would come to encompass sisters, nature, and God's entire family. In Assisi society, Clare was renowned for her physical beauty; now her years of charity and service had generated the reputation of her spiritual beauty as well. Francis heard of her light and grace and desired that she live his way of life. Clare's heart had been converted long ago; now her entire life was ripening toward outward conversion. The young noblewoman continued to refuse offers of marriage and was feeling great pressure from her family. Marriage was an important factor in securing the stability of her noble house, and to that end Clare was a very valuable asset. Like Francis, a decision would have to be made. He took the lead, courting her to a very different life, one that she sought, the true life she always dreamed of.

Throughout the year 1211, Francis and Clare met secretly – Clare always accompanied by a woman friend, and Francis by a brother.

Francis went many times to preach to her, so that Clare acquiesced to his preaching, renounced the world and all earthly things, and went to serve God as soon as she was able.

—Acts of the Process of Canonization of Clare, XII, 2

A WEDDING OF SOULS

"As soon as she was able" came the following year, when Clare turned eighteen. After a year of sharing the pleasure of each other's company; after sharing her innermost self with her intimate friend; after discussing all his hopes over candlelight; everything made sense now! All the events and qualities of her life had lead up to this, the event that had been unnamed and shrouded until now, but which had become crystal clear through the light in Francis's eyes. Christ had reached out to Clare through the likeness of Francis, and she was now able to take his hand. And like any adolescent girl, there were exciting signs and symbols and plans for her impending journey:

The father Francis told her that on the day of the feast [Palm Sunday], she should go dressed and adorned, together with the crowd of people, to church to receive a palm. . . . Therefore, when Sunday came, the young girl, radiant with festive splendor among the crowd of women, entered the church with the others.

As the others were going to receive their palms, Clare remained in her place out of shyness. Seeing this, the Bishop, coming down the steps, came to her and placed a palm in her hand.

—THOMAS OF CELANO, *The Life of St. Clare*

Clare left her home quietly the following night, her young heart pounding both with excitement and the fear of being discovered. She left through what was called the "door of the dead," a small door at the end of a long, narrow hallway in her home. This was a common feature in Umbrian houses and is thought to be the hallway through which the deceased were carried out in their coffins. For Clare's journey, it was appropriate somehow – she was dying to her old life and would journey through this transforming corridor, with its new life waiting on the other side of the door.

Every rite of passage both links and divides the past and future; it is like an air-lock, and the symbolic journey through this airlock ushers us into an enlargement of spirit. It is one of the hallmarks of it that there is no way back, growth cannot be ungrown, the old ways have become impossible. The airlock is a one-way passage. So it is a true death and a genuine rebirth through which we enter a new relationship with our own story. . . .

—SR. FRANCES TERESA, OSC, *This Living Mirror:*
Reflections on Clare of Assisi

Clare opened the door, stepped over that threshold and out of her childhood forever. She stood on the piazza in a darkness that must have seemed both overwhelming and expectant with the stardust of life, the starkness of death, and the brightness of the mystery of all God's fireflies. She had an appointment to keep – a secret rendezvous with the gentle midwife of her soul – and so departed through the Arazzo gate of Assisi and began to run to the Porziuncula, the tiny stone chapel of St. Mary of the Angels that Francis had rebuilt and loved so dearly.

This small, intimate chapel is cherished not only because it is where Francis and his brothers lived in early community; it is also the place at which Clare was joined to Francis for life, together in their love of God.

For Clare, it was the wedding chapel of her soul.

For Francis, it would become the place at which he wished to depart this life.

Clare ran to the Porziuncula. Waiting to receive her, Francis and the brothers were keeping watch and observing sacred vigils by candlelight.

Clare found her way through the darkness to the chapel. The brothers came to welcome her, the light of candles illuminating the night, the light of love illuminating their eyes. And there at the altar was Francis, her Bridegroom.

There, in this intimate place, surrounded by love, Clare was consecrated as the first Franciscan woman, taking her lifelong vows of love of God, poverty, and chastity. Like Francis before her, she surrendered her fine clothes and was given a sackcloth robe and a belt of cord.

For my wedding, I will dress in black
And never again will I look back
Ah, my dark angels we must part
For I've made a sanctuary of my heart
To want what I have
To take what I'm given with grace
For this I pray
On my wedding day
For my wedding, I don't want violins
Or sentimental songs about thick and thin
I want a moment of silence and a moment of prayer
For the love we'll need to make it in the world out there
To want what we have
To take what we're given with grace
For these things I pray
On my wedding day

—LARRY JOHN MACNALLY, "For My Wedding"

Then Clare knelt before God and offered to Francis with joy the very symbol of her worldly glory: her long, golden hair. Francis himself cut that wonderful hair, gently and lovingly, in a ritual that symbolized both her wedding to God through Francis, and the mutual sexual sacrifice of the wedding night.

37

In the Christmas story "The Gift of the Magi" by O. Henry, a poor husband and wife surrender their most valued treasures, unbeknownst to each other, to buy their beloved spouses the perfect Christmas gift. On Christmas Eve, the husband sells his gold watch to buy his wife combs for her hair; his wife cuts and sells her knee-length tresses to the wigmaker so that she can buy her husband a beautiful watch chain. They meet to exchange gifts and stand there with a chain and combs that cannot be worn – but that are more valuable than the objects they no longer possess. The couple, like Francis and Clare, gave up their favorite treasures on earth for the greatest gift they already shared: true love.

A RISK FOR LOVE

And so Francis gave Clare the tonsure, the shaven head or "crown" worn by monks. She surrendered a worldly beauty for which she was known to stand with him; Francis cut away the very thing he loved, enjoyed, and gazed upon. They did this for divine love. And after a life of living alone in her spirituality, Francis, beginning with himself, also gave Clare the most precious gift of like-minded souls: a community.

The reception and investiture of Clare made her at once a spiritual daughter, spouse, and colleague to Francis. But this is where Francis took a tremendous risk for the first Franciscan woman: he simply had no authority to witness her act of profession, her vows. That role was reserved for bishops, especially in the case of a noblewoman. Francis was not and never intended to be even a priest. He and his brothers could have been arrested that night for their interaction with Clare, the entire Franciscan movement halted right then and there. But to Francis, welcoming Clare's light into their life was simply the right thing to do.

The dreamlike wedding experience of Clare's initiation would soon be jolted back into reality. For her immediate safety, she was taken to San Paolo, a Benedictine church across the Tescio River. Why for safety? Clare had acted in the same manner as Mary's "yes" to God: she made a decision of faith and like Mary was now in real danger. (In Mary's time, it was customary, even lawful, to stone a woman to death for being unfaithful, or, as in her case, unmarried and pregnant.)

When Clare's family finally discovered what she had done, they came after her. The men in her family found her at San Paolo, confronted her in the church, and tried in every way to berate and counteract her decision. They were there to bring her home, even by coercion if necessary. Finally they came after her physically. Clare ran up onto the altar for sanctuary. They would respect that holy boundary and do her no harm.

There she unveiled to her kinsmen her shorn head – and the gravity of her decision. When they saw the concrete sign of her commitment, they let her go.

HE OBEYED

. . . Francis saw *something in Clare, he* believed, and obeyed – *taking her into his fraternity – and that allowed her to become Mary to his Elizabeth.*

—JOSEPH P. CHINNICI, *Contemporary Reflections on the Spirituality of Clare*

When we hear the words "obey" or "obedience" in our western culture, we tend to recoil, often with a sense of distaste or displeasure. We, stalwart in our rugged individualism, have been instructed somehow that obedience is negative, an action (or rather, inaction) of self-denial or submission to another's will, carrying a loss or debasement of personal identity. The words "to love, honor, and obey" have long been stricken from the marriage ceremony and replaced by more comfortable terms often created by the engaged couple. And while writing our own vows can be an emotionally fulfilling and personal experience, there is a reason why certain words have been chosen in an attempt to capture the deeply spiritual and sacramental aspects of relationship, of bonds that unite us to each other as heaven unites with earth.

It may be a cosmic coincidence that the word "obey," like Francis himself, has its roots in the thirteenth century. It comes from the Old French *obeir* and from the Latin *oboedire* – to "pay attention to; to give ear; to listen to."

Although the word has taken on quite a different connotation in our language, obedience is not mere submission to another's will. When we obey, we are listening – truly listening – to another.

We can utilize the habitual spousal replies that we have learned over the years, when our husband or wife is irritated or agitated about life, money, work. Or, we can listen . . . and hear our best friend struggling toward a life full of meaning and peace, and the fear that it will be in vain.

We can employ the usual parental replies, when our teenager is angry with us, or we can listen and hear her frustration in fragility, remember our own, and discern in time a proper and genuine response to nourish a young soul's journey.

When we obey in this original sense, it is as though we are listening with the ear of the Spirit. Obedience awakens us from the sleepiness of role playing; it liberates us and helps us to be truly in relationship as our higher selves. Obedience delivers us from taking things personally. It generates grace and dignity, for ourselves and for our loved ones.

Francis listened to God. He was obedient to God. He made a decision that sat very well with heaven, if not with society and local authorities. He invited Clare, his best friend and counter-part, to share his calling and journey because he recognized her calling and journey. Francis did not lose himself in his obedience, as is the customary concern. To the contrary: he met his destiny.

Soon Francis gave to Clare San Damiano, the first church he had rebuilt so carefully. This would be the young girl's home and enclosure until her death at sixty-one. There, as her faith grew, she too would be given companions: Agnese, Filippa, Giacama, Benvenuta, Lucia, Pacifica. Eventually her own mother, sister, and later nieces would join her in community, bestowing upon Clare a wonderful emotional comfort and spiritual treasure on this earth: they would serve the poor together, as family.

THE WITNESS

That was the mystery of it all, the divine becoming human. It started with Jesus, and Francis made it real for [Clare] and for all his brothers and sisters. That was Clare's gift from [Francis] who had loved God so intensely and perfectly that he ended up loving her. Only one who loves God above all can love a woman as she should be loved, selflessly, totally, with God's own love enfleshed in a poor little man.

—MURRAY BODO, OFM, *Clare: A Light in the Garden*

Francis did not create Clare's love of God, nor did he implant her spiritual nature. He gave witness to them, which was all she needed to soar like the larks he loved so dearly. He helped deliver her to her true self, which had been shining as best as possible from under the bushel basket of her affluence. Clare had a good family and friends, but in Francis she found a partner in Christ, in life, in divine and eternal love.

In a sacramental marriage, the spouse is an intimate witness – like the Holy Spirit – an advocate, friend, and counselor. Spouses will witness all things in each other during their life together:

good times and bad, losses and victories, growth, change, pain, joy, aging, health, sickness. Should one become critically ill, even grown children will be asked to leave a hospital room. But the spouse will remain. The spouse will see his or her partner through all things, even unto the end – a witness and living record of a life.

INTIMACY

Of course Francis and Clare never married in the worldly sense; Francis lived in community with his brothers and Clare at her convent with her community. They never consummated their relationship. Still they mirror to us a powerful example of potent romance and sexuality. The Christian marriage vow includes a promise to love the spouse "forsaking all others," and Francis and Clare were able to do this, I believe, because they brought the thirteenth-century concept of courtly love to the religious life.

What they created was a sense of enclosure, not only in the religious sense of enclosure, or cloister, but between them as two people in love. They held God first in their heart and vision; then they held each other. For Francis, there was God and Clare; for Clare, there was God and Francis, often intermingled. It has been said that for most of his life, the only woman's face Francis allowed himself to know completely was Clare's. He would not gaze on another.

Much of their passion, perseverance, and success would come from this central point of enclosure, of being turned to each other, forsaking all others, all earthly options, all worldly distractions, both wills rooted in the love and service of God. Placing our spouse or partner beside our image of God creates the basis for a permanent longing and intimacy, because in the end, our desire for each other is our desire for God. Francis and Clare modeled this for us, spiritually, romantically, sexually, faithfully.

Of course, we might say, it was easy for Francis and Clare to accomplish this ideal in their day – there were no electronic media, no television, no magazines or teasing tabloids, no perpetual parade of enticing images, no daily invitations to stray quietly via the Internet in the course of their work. And you would be right. These are the special challenges of today's couples, and indeed these can be painful challenges if both spouses do not share the same enjoyment or vision of enclosed sexuality. But the larger problem facing today's couples may be something even more insidious, something we have not yet begun to name and explore. Marriage is the one union that is fully sanctioned and encouraged in all manner of shared physicality, sexuality, and procreation. A kiss for luck! Mazel tov! The rice is thrown, the glass is shattered. And yet, this is the relationship that is not eroticized in our culture. Even worse, marriage can be perceived as a loss of sexuality.

It is well known that the divorce rate in the United States skyrocketed in recent decades, increasing to more than 50 percent in the 1990s for first-time marriages. Concurrently, it has also been discerned in various studies that the age at which most Americans reach emotional maturity has increased to thirty-two. That number represents twice the time it takes to reach physical maturity. Factors like the "trial" approach to marriage and a postponed adulthood may certainly affect the rate of divorce; however, there may be a deeper issue involved, regarding our imagination for marriage – and our ability to maintain an intimate sense of enclosure in our day-in-day-out interactions.

When we first encounter our special love, our soul mate, it is as though the universe has opened up to shower down upon us the promise of God and all his magic. Through the veil of our ordinary life, we see a glimpse of the whole of sparkling creation and the mirror of our heart's innermost wishes. We have dared to dream, we think, and the rush of our soul and the butterflies alighting through our solar plexus tell us, This love I have sought is true, it is possible! I have seen it, the miracle! And we become like children again, discovering, or rediscovering, the spells of life and love, and dandelion clocks, and chocolate-covered raspberry rings, and twilight, and the stars, and the timeless and eternal sea. Everything is reborn into sacred symbols and shrines – trinkets in antique stores, flowers, songs, candlelight, stories, books, cafés, riverside benches – the whole universe sings a love song to us, and we return the refrain in kind.

When we have come together for some time, and we engage in the creation of a life and home and a family, most of us enter into a tangible world of concrete needs that require constant, and seemingly unending, attention. After some years of working, and homemaking, and childrearing, with little time free and little time together, we may ask, *Where did the universe go? Everything seems so small....*

Fear not. The life at hand is the living-out of the miracle of the gift of love. We just may lose sight of the horizon when so steeped in the thoroughfare.

In his book *The Four Loves*, C. S. Lewis discerns and explores in distinct chapters the types of love that operate in specific ways throughout life: *eros,* or romantic love; *storge,* or affection "as that of parents for children"; *philia,* or friendship; and *agape,* the love of God, which Lewis calls charity. What couples need to recall, teach, underscore, and celebrate is that all these loves are found together operating within a good marriage.

Francis and Clare loved each other and created and managed households. When challenged in their daily lives, their inspiration did not cease, and their faith did not falter. Perhaps the distance they kept from each other in fact helped them to retain the spark of their love, to keep their interactions charged and fresh as the years passed. When I studied theology at Maryknoll School of Theology in New York, I knew a sister who shared the best thought on celibacy I have ever heard.

"Celibacy is not about never falling in love," said Sr. Geri Hable. "It's about falling in love over and over and over again."

Did she mean falling in love with different people she encountered during the years of her ministry?

Did she mean falling in love over and over with God?

Or did she mean falling in love over and over with her vocation, choosing her ministry again and again, when presented with
other options for her life? Chances are she meant all of these.

The love of God, of a person, and of a vocation applies to us
all. Marriage is also a vocation, a calling. This is a great gift, to
be able to keep choosing our relationship, our marriage, and our
life – regardless of its demands, whirlwind busyness, routine or
familiarity. It is Love.

EROS AND A DREAM OF FRANCIS

Francis and Clare shared exquisite understanding of the sacrificial
and liberating nature of love, as they shared exquisite understanding of the sacrificial and liberating nature of the Cross: God is at
the center. In Clare's correspondence to Agnes of Prague, daughter
of the king of Bohemia, whose conversion she sought and eventually won, Clare's portrayal of the divine love demonstrates the happy
contradictions of a world turned upside down by God, similar to
the promises of the "Magnificat," and the "Prayer Attributed to St.
Francis":

> *When you have loved Him, you shall be chaste; when you have touched Him,*
> *You shall become pure; when you have accepted Him, you shall be a virgin.*
> *Whose power is stronger,*
> *Whose generosity is more abundant,*
> *Whose appearance more beautiful,*
> *Whose love more tender,*

Whose courtesy more gracious.
In whose embrace you are already caught up;
Who has adorned your breast with precious stones
And has placed priceless pearls in your ears
And has surrounded you with sparkling gems
As though blossoms of springtime
And placed on your head a golden crown
As a sign [to all] of your holiness.

—ST. CLARE OF ASSISI, First Letter to Agnes of Prague, 8-11

Further, the paradox that Clare pens in the beginning lines above creates the image of a searing union with God, a love that propels us from the over-trod world of red-hot distraction higher up into the blue-hot burning of a different flame. Here Clare's words are reminiscent of the Song of Songs – her vivid images of springtime and glorious gems, surpassing beauty, power and intimacy, and the crown all indicate her natural appreciation of the senses and all their gifts.

Perhaps that is not of great surprise. Clare's love for Francis was, of course, love of a flesh-and-blood man as well as for the imitator of Christ, and for Christ himself. But Clare was able to engage her feelings and propel her love for Francis to a higher level.

Although we traditionally hold an image of Francis as "an instrument of peace," the reality was that his unebbing libido could be a source of rage to him. One story has it, in fact, that he was so full of self-loathing regarding his human desires that once he dragged himself through the rose bushes in the garden of the Porziuncula – hoping that the painful thorns would both quell him and perhaps "tear" the desire from his flesh.

"Sometimes God's greatest gift is unanswered prayers," goes the country song. And perhaps Francis needed to accept that his desire for human contact and his desire for God were the same passion; that is, if his human drive and desire were expunged somehow, so would his desire to forge his mission of compassion be expunged. Here again we look to Clare for help – help in embracing our dualities and the contradiction of life-through-death. She too was human. Clare had a dream of Francis that she shared, because she was proud of it.

Clare dreamed that she was going up a staircase. Francis was at the top, on the landing. As she got nearer to him, he parted his cassock, exposing his body to her. Indicating his torso, he said, "Come, drink, my virgin." Clare put her mouth to his nipple and drank. When she drew away from him, she found that his nipple had remained in her mouth, but that it had changed to gold. She removed it, turned it around, and saw in its mirror the reflection of her own face.

Clare's powerful, transcendent dream of Francis integrated the categories of erotic love and spirituality in a manner that was beneficial to her life and fueling to her faith. In it, Francis was Lover, Father, Mother, Mirror, the one who gives the milk of life for her sake. The appearance of her own reflection in the dream is also key. That she saw herself demonstrates that she was becoming self-actualized, and was capable and called to offer all those nurturing roles as well. As with Francis, her sexual love as a woman would not be expunged – only developed to connect with God's divine love. She would retain this important aspect of her humanity, bringing into unison the flesh and the spirit in peace and harmony.

It has often been said that Clare loved Francis: of course she did; had he not kindled in her soul a twin flame of the love of God from that burning in his own, each flame adding something to the other?

—NESTA DE ROBECK, *St. Clare of Assisi*

SHE OBEYED

We understand humility to mean knowledge of oneself, with the modesty or respectfulness to accept our limitations, the things we cannot do; but humility also means owning and utilizing the things we can do. This can be a challenge for women even today. Following is a heartening, even amusing, exchange between a pope, Gregory IX, and Clare, a woman of God. Just as Francis obeyed and created a miracle, so would Clare need to emerge from her feminine shyness into the true humility of womanhood – and facilitate her own miracle. This story comes from the *Fioretti*, *The Little Flowers of St. Francis*:

St. Clare, most devoted disciple of the Cross of Christ and noble plant of St. Francis, was of such sanctity, that not only bishops and cardinals but the Pope himself desired, with great affection, to see and to hear her, and oftentimes visited her in person.

Once when the Holy Father went to her convent, to hear her speak of heaven-ly and divine things; whilst they were together, holding divers [sic] discourses, St. Clare meanwhile had the tables prepared, and the loaves placed on them in order that the Holy Father might bless them. The spiritual discourse being ended, she inclined herself with great reverence, prayed him to be pleased to bless the loaves of her repast. The Holy Father answered, "Sister Clare, most true and faithful one, I desire that thou bless these loaves, and make on them the sign of the most holy Cross, to which thou has entirely given thyself."

St. Clare replied, "Most Holy Father, pardon me, who would be worthy of too great rebuke, if before the Vicar of Christ, I, who am a worthless woman, should presume to give this blessing."

And the Pope answered, "In order that this may not be imputed to presump-tion but to the merit of obedience, I command thee by holy obedience that thou make on these loaves the sign of the most holy Cross, and bless them in the name of God."

Then St. Clare, like a true daughter of obedience, most devoutly blessed these loaves with the sign of the most holy Cross.

Wonderful to relate! Immediately there appeared on all the loaves the sign of the cross most beautifully figured; then of these loaves, some were eaten and some were preserved. The Holy Father, having seen the miracle, took some of the loaves with him and departed, leaving St. Clare with his blessing.

—The Little Flowers of St. Francis, XXXII

Both Francis and Clare had their miracles. Bread – the staple of life, and of Christ's meal, pulled together from the wheat of the earth, from water, yeast, warmth, and the effort of human hands – was Clare's miracle, a spiritual food to be shared in community.

> The flour in the sack is soft –
> a powdered silk. It is beautiful.
> It has become this way
> because it was harvested, because
> it was threshed, and then milled.
> Here is the terror of Autumn.
> And the beauty! What is ripe is
> sacrificed. Torn loose. The grain
> is wrestled from the plant, from everything
> familiar. We must expect this to happen
> to ourselves. I want to know this in you . . .
> that you have been on the threshing floor.
> I need you to see that I have been
> between the grinding stones. It will make us
> careful of each other, of all grain.
> The flour in the sack is soft –
> a powdered silk. How terrible is beauty.
> How full of sacrifice and grace.
> Let us honor all that has dared
> to grow to fruition.

—GUNILLA MORRIS, "Autumn," *Becoming Bread*

POVERTY OF SPIRIT

Each year saw the number of brothers double. They were coming in now
from all directions, and some of them were destined to play an important
role in one of the greatest adventures in Christian thought. Even more
sensitive than the men to a mystical call, the women at San Damiano
sought the inner peace that a turbulent, violent world threatened to
destroy. . . . A song of joy went up to heaven. This was a moment never
quite recaptured later. The bolt from the blue can't be repeated.

—JULIEN GREEN, *God's Fool*

The rise of Francis's brotherhood, the First Order of St. Francis, was meteoric. Franciscan spirituality was a cleansing gust of wind during the time of a medieval church as ornate and ensconced as a Fabergé egg. Men found it irresistible, this invitation to a pared-down experience of actually living like Christ and his disciples, without possessions and liberated to serve all.

The charged presence of Clare made it a holistic experience of spirituality for them – not one lived above, below, or in avoidance of half the world's population. By 1215, the Second Order of St. Francis, the Poor Clares, was in place. Both orders would travel and initiate the development of new houses in other cities in Italy, across Europe, England, and Ireland.

Soon the Third Order of St. Francis would evolve, an important secular order that would encourage the laity to live more closely to their spirituality, thereby integrating their faith in daily life. All these orders remain strong with us today.

Francis and Clare, both devoted to Holy Poverty, lived out their calling in deep humility and constant service among the poor, the sick, and the ostracized. Francis and Clare saw with crystal clarity, and from their own experience, that although wealth may lead to more wealth, poverty would lead to spiritual treasure.

Francis and Clare strove daily to keep their hands empty, to borrow the imagery of St. Augustine, so that they would be better able to receive and do God's will. They shared the understanding that poverty is not merely surrendering the things of this world; true poverty is about turning one's will to God. That is where real poverty lies. And that is why Jesus moved them so: his utter humility and obedience to God, beginning with his humble birth in the straw of a manger. Clare too would sleep on a little straw bed herself, gathered on the stone floor of her dormitory. "Blessed are the poor in spirit," for they will answer God's invitation with trust and joy and freedom, in love.

Francis and Clare shared this, in the same time and place, the unique understanding of the power, necessity, and loveliness of poverty. For them it was the key to the gateway of the kingdom of God. It comforted and inspired Francis to have such a witness in Clare, someone who in her way would become his vision of Lady Poverty. They preached and wrote constantly about poverty and charity, setting out to convert or reawaken the hearts of men and women in Europe and the Near East. They especially enjoyed seeking the conversion of nobility, who often responded to their heartfelt and genuine invitations to abandon their trappings for liberation of spirit, freedom to love, and resurrected life. Their writings demonstrate also that their sacrifice did not drain or tire them; rather it fueled them with energy, joy, and radiance:

What a great and laudable exchange:
To leave the things of time for those of eternity
To choose the things of heaven for the goods of earth
To receive the hundred-fold in place of one,
And to possess a blessed and eternal life.

—CLARE OF ASSISI, First Letter to Agnes of Prague, 30

Happy indeed is she to whom it is given to share this sacred banquet,
To cling with all her heart to Him
Whose beauty all the heavenly hosts admire unceasingly,
Whose love inflames our love,
Whose contemplation is our refreshment,
Whose graciousness is our joy,
Whose gentleness fills us to overflowing,
Whose remembrance brings a gentle light,
Whose fragrance will revive the dead,
Whose glorious vision will be the happiness
 of all the citizens of the heavenly Jerusalem.

—CLARE OF ASSISI, Fourth Letter to Agnes of Prague, 9-13

SISTER DEATH

Toward the end of my visit in Assisi, I took a walk in Clare's convent and admired the courtyard garden for a moment. Soon I sensed someone beside me. I turned my head and saw an old woman, close to eighty, another traveler, tall, slim, and well dressed. We stood in silence for a time. Then, as happens in such a place of pilgrimage, we began to chat – about Francis, about the city then and now, about Clare's hair. Soon we grew silent once more and paused there, simply sharing the joyful presence of this meaningful place. Then her expression turned more serious. She turned to me again.

"I am getting older," she explained. "And I am at a stage in my life when I am, well, beginning to wrap things up."

I listened. She continued.

"And one of the things I am doing is going through my belongings and discerning where things should go, and with whom. I have something that I would like to give you, if you don't mind," she said. "I have a sense about you, and I would like the right thing to be with the right person. Is that all right with you?"

I looked at her face, her fine wrinkled skin, her fading blue eyes.

"Yes, of course," I answered, and gave her my address back in the States. We said nothing more about it. I had forgotten about our exchange when, two months later, a small package wrapped in brown paper arrived in the mail bearing the gift of a first-class relic of St. Clare of Assisi, encased in glass and silver, closed with the Vatican seal.

❧

Both Francis and Clare would suffer physically from the hardships of their lives. Clare would be ill for many years, and Francis would eventually lose his eyesight. (Clare would become the patroness of sore eyes.) By today's standards, he died very young, only forty-four years old. He had struggled with fever and pain for seven weeks before he departed this life on October 3, 1226.

His life had been a constant letting-go, and Clare in turn would let him go. She knew this further letting-go would be hard and that winter was threatening the hillside where she lived. She could not think of that. Instead she looked up at Brother Sun and let Francis go and surrendered, for she knew that she would rise again, even from this . . . even from this.

—MURRAY BODO, OFM, *Clare: A Light in the Garden*

The funeral procession up to Assisi was one of triumph with songs and waving olive branches and lighted candles. When it reached San Damiano the brothers paused . . . "lifted the body from the bier, and held it in their raised arms in front of the window so long as my Lady Clare and the other sisters wished for their comfort."

—NESTA DE ROBECK, *St. Clare of Assisi*

Twenty-seven years after Francis's death, Clare died as she lived – simply – in the place where she slept during her forty-two years at San Damiano, the stone floor of her sweet small dormitory.

Even in death she embodies Francis's ideal: there is no marker to call attention to the spot where the dear lady departed this life, no plaque or painting or shrine.

There may be the warmth of a few humble flowers, though, on the cold stone floor, placed there by a knowing stranger, a loving witness across time.

THE UNION OF SOULS

Francis and Clare dared to grow to fruition. They would remain blessed throughout their lives with brothers and sisters, hard work, strong faith, serious challenges, and a miracle here and there. Most of all they had each other on the way to Christ. Francis and Clare were a New Adam and New Eve, best friends, counterparts, holy mirrors whose reflection showed each other – and us – a glimpse of the infinite radiance of God. They took a lifetime to learn to love . . . as Christ loved us.

At last, it is difficult to discern where Francis ends and Clare begins, when reading their final blessings to their brothers and sisters, present and future. So close, their spirits dovetail, and their words soar in their last known wishes for us.

I, brother Francis, the little one, wish to follow the life and poverty of our most high Lord Jesus Christ and of his most holy mother and to persevere in this until the end; and I will ask and counsel you, my ladies, to live always in this most holy life and in poverty.

—FRANCIS OF ASSISI, *Last Will for Clare and Her Sisters*, 1-2

I, Clare, a handmaid of Christ, a little plant of our holy father Francis, a sister and mother of you and the other Poor Sisters, although unworthy, ask our Lord Jesus Christ through his mercy and through the intercession of his most holy Mother Mary, of Blessed Michael the Archangel and all the angels of God, and of all his men and women saints, that the heavenly Father give you and confirm for you this most holy blessing . . .

—CLARE OF ASSISI, *The Blessing Attributed to St. Clare*, 5-7

And whoever shall have observed these things, may he be filled in heaven with the blessing of the most high Father and on earth with the blessing of His beloved Son, with the most Holy Spirit the Paraclete, and with all the powers of heaven and all the saints.

—FRANCIS OF ASSISI, *Testament*, 40

On earth, may he increase His grace and virtues among His servants and hand-maids . . . In heaven, may He exalt and glorify you in His Church Triumphant among all His men and women saints.

—CLARE OF ASSISI, *The Blessing Attributed to St. Clare*, 8-9

I, little brother Francis, your servant, inasmuch as I can, confirm for you this most holy blessing both within and without . . .

—FRANCIS OF ASSISI, *Testament*, 41

. . . I bless all my brothers, those who are in the Order, and those who will come until the end of the world. Let them always love and be faithful to our Lady Holy Poverty . . .

—FRANCIS OF ASSISI, *Testament of Siena, 1, 4*

I bless you in my life and after my death as much as I can, and more than I can, with all the blessings with which the Father of mercies has and will have blessed His sons and daughters in heaven and on earth.

—CLARE OF ASSISI, *The Blessing Attributed to St. Clare*

THE INHERITANCE

[Y]ou see the grain-fields down yonder? I do not eat bread. Wheat is of no use to me. The wheat fields have nothing to say to me. And that is sad. But you have hair that is the color of gold. Think how wonderful that will be when you have tamed me! The grain, which is also golden, will bring me back the thought of you. And I shall love to listen to the wind in the wheat. . . .

—ANTOINE DE ST. EXUPÉRY, *The Fox, The Little Prince*

It has been said that Francis asked a brother to collect the tresses of shorn hair that had fallen to the ground on the altar the night Clare was made the first Franciscan woman – and that Francis held on to Clare's sacrifice, her beautiful long hair, for the rest of his life. It has even been reported that he kept her golden locks on his person, close to his heart. What were once simple human strands had become sacred, a precious heirloom, through his love for her.

Throughout Clare's life at San Damiano, there hung the cross of the poor Jesus that first "spoke" to Francis at the beginning of his spiritual journey. It remained at Clare's convent, above the altar, throughout the blossoming of the Franciscan orders. Today it hangs above Clare's crypt at her basilica in Assisi. Francis must have desired that this treasure remain with Clare, his counterpart, after his death; his brothers would present it with grateful hearts, especially for her critical guidance to the communities after Francis died. Clare was an inspiration to Francis as he lived; her example of actually living his rule of life kept him going when his own strength, or that of his brothers, faltered. Mother Clare kept the vision of Francis vibrant and alive, even after his departure, by guiding and strengthening all their spiritual children.

Finally, Francis's very garments, his sackcloth clothes, also lie within the enclosure of Clare's basilica. He had given his worldly clothes to his father; to Clare he would give the few belongings of their shared life in God and Love. All these things remained precious. As with any great love between a man and a woman, these simple effects held all the beauty, meaning, and memory that could be bestowed upon a worldly item. And Clare was his beneficiary, his beloved next-of-kin. With God as the creator and center of their love,

Clare gives depth to his sacramental belief. She becomes the human instrument which teaches [Francis] the necessity of practicing solidarity with everything created that bears the mark of the Spirit: errant brothers, a sinful church . . . the water and the wine on the altar, his own frail body . . . and the broken man on the cross.

—JOSEPH P. CHINNICI, *Contemporary Reflections on the Spirituality of Clare*

Is this not the very purpose and result of a model marriage – to perceive and love the image of God in each other, and from this inspired center, generate love outward to children, brothers, sisters, and community? Both heaven and earth are blessed when such a union celebrates, remembers, and practices the sacred among all their surroundings and company.

This is the meaning of sacrament. This is the essence and image of the inspired marriage: not managing the household, not growing old together, not sex, not even children – although all these are exceptional blessings – but rather the continued revered bond that acts as the anchor, center, and axis around which all things revolve, the window through which all of life is perceived and met, for whatever time we have together. So in love, Francis and Clare would come to praise the sacrament in all things.

In his renowned "Canticle of Brother Sun," we experience Francis's deep love for God and nature, and enjoy all the brother-sister imagery that his enlightened soul was able to evoke. Of particular pertinence here is praise of Sister Moon and the stars, "shining and precious and fair," or *chiarite e belle*, in Italian. Here Clare's name, Chiara, is revealed – for to Francis she was a shining and precious star, his lady, his partner, and his friend.

All praise be yours, my Lord, through all that you have made,
And first my Lord, Brother Sun, who brings the day;
And light you give to us through him.
Of you, Most High, he bears likeness.
All praise be yours, my Lord, for Sister Moon
And the stars; in heaven you have made them,
Shining and precious and fair.

—FRANCIS OF ASSISI

Love Notes

What We Can Learn from Francis and Clare

Rites of Passage

Francis and Clare exhibited the kind of jarring transition, moving from the childhood home of their parents to that of their young adulthood, as we can see with our kids today. We in the west do not have very supportive rites of passage in place for our teens and young adults. Meaningful moments parents celebrate include the acquisition of a driver's license, turning 18, and graduation from high school. But so much of a teen's vital personal growth occurs alone, with other friends or adults, or even in secret, as in the case of Clare. This can pertain to sexual development as well as spiritual development. Why the hiding?

Clearly the pressure of "behaving" while going through these often difficult transitions is on the child, not the parent. That is, it is all right to grow up – just don't get in trouble, fight, use inappropriate language, become confused, embarrass, or otherwise step out of line.

On one hand, it is necessary and helpful for teens to "test out" their adult self through friendships with teachers, coaches, clergy, and other adults who can serve as nonjudgmental mentors.

However, long-term growth and peace with family members will depend on how the parents react to their children growing up; that is, how the parents behave during this transition.

Parents are capable of a broad expanse of emotions when faced with the onset of their children's maturity – experiencing fear, helplessness, sadness, even anger – and can respond to their teenager's distance or confrontation with knee-jerk reactions that, although understandable, do not support or nurture either person.

With God at the center of a parent's life, through spirituality, prayer, and other forms of communion, we can respond to our children supportively through the simple action of taking our sense of overarching authority out of the equation. Our children are part of us and belong to us, certainly, and we are responsible for them. But as Francis and Clare demonstrate so clearly, our children truly belong to God, and God works directly in their lives in a way that we would do well to observe, honor, and obey.

Myth

As with the family, all love relationships contain a story, a true myth – meeting, falling in love, marriage, geographical moves, leaps of faith, work, pivotal events that propelled us, great friends, additions to the family, and so on. This is great mythology, real adventure. Couples need to keep their myth alive, recalling it, even ritualizing it, and adding to it as the epic evolves, to keep the symbols full of meaning. Try writing your own story as a book, recalling as many details as possible. Include photos and souvenirs such as theater tickets to illustrate. Capture the essence of your story; then pass the book on to your children.

Also, studies indicate that successful couples celebrate more than one anniversary. They celebrate their wedding anniversary, for example, plus another special day: the day they met, their first date, their first kiss, or another event that brought them together. And they celebrate these two (or more) anniversaries every year. It makes sense: the wedding is usually an event shared with family and friends. It is an outward sign, to and with community. But the "other" anniversary, the private one, is meant just for the couple to know and share. This is the moment, the treasure, that continues to fuel the romance, the essence of the relationship that keeps it vibrant.

Like any couple, Francis and Clare had many such moments: their year of conversations on the wonders of life, their future, and the love of God; the consecration of Clare, their "wedding night"; the meals they shared; the friends they made. These joys certainly were remembered and celebrated in their hearts. Just recalling their special days with joy fuels our hearts as well.

Risk

Francis and Clare showed us how a step toward divine love required risk, when she left her home in secret to join Francis and he risked the entire Franciscan community to receive her.

There is an element of risk in life, especially when we strive actively toward happiness. So many couples hope and plan and wish for their life to evolve in one way or another. They dream of starting a business, moving to Alaska, or taking a year off to travel the world. The years pass. It is natural to put safety first, especially in these uncertain times. But love will require a leap of faith for the vivid life of dreams. Make a journey for your soul. Take your chances. And don't wait for every detail to be nailed down. Trust in God and in yourself. Meet your miracles halfway.

Mirrors

Francis and Clare clearly saw God in each other, and they were mirrors to each other; therefore they reflected the best in each other. All spouses are mirrors to each other. How do we mirror our spouse, our counterpart, in our relationship? Do we mirror him or her with positive regard, humor, hope, and the gravity of a loving witness? Consider if this has changed with time, for better or worse, and how the mirror might be cleaned, or polished, or restored with simple practice of daily awareness.

Then, at the surface of the mirror, consider the holy humility, the blessed poverty, the untold labors and burdens that he endured for the redemption of the whole human race.

—CLARE OF ASSISI, *Fourth Letter to Agnes*, 22

The mirror was an intrinsic part of the spiritual practice of Clare, and she referred to it often as a tool in her reflections and correspondence. When guiding those under her direction to look into the spiritual mirror, she used the lovely word *considerare*, which has a meaning closer to star-gazing.

Gazing with wonder as we do at the night sky and all its mysteries, we gaze into the mystery of our life and see beyond the mirror's immediate reflection. We see our journey, the many people who have touched our lives, our discarded failures, and our hope and role in a starry universe. Looking deeper into the mirror, we see the vision expand. We see how it is the pattern of the stars themselves to be born, to live, and to shine their brightest when they die. We see love as the very fabric of creation.

Cornerstones

When Francis rebuilt the chapel at San Damiano, he kept some of the old stones, and he added new ones to rebuild and bolster the structure. Consider your relationship as a building, a stone castle, or a chapel. What good old stones form the foundation of your relationship, your marriage? Do they remain true and strong cornerstones? What stones have become weak or broken? Consider what may repair or replace them, if you desire, and how.

Thresholds

When Clare left her home through the "door of the dead" she crossed a threshold through which there was no turning back. When we embark on our own journey into love, we too cross a threshold and move forward into a new life in a new way. Meet it wholeheartedly. Attempting to retain our former life and identity once we enter into love may diminish our new life and intimacy with our partner. The way to divine love is to surrender to new life. Trust the invitation of the threshold that it is the manner and way of all growth and life throughout creation.

Marriage is a priesthood shared by two –
with all the joys, passions, challenges, and mysteries
two entwined lives can hold.

—*Dear Little One: Thoughts to My Child*
in an Uncertain World

❖

Grass waving, a green hammock, a breezy cradle of bees.
Stone slabs stand, split by a vertical ray.
You had better walk the wave. Walk the wave –
don't hurt your feet.
In the wave's embrace you never know you are drowning.
And then He comes. He lays his yoke on your back.
You feel it, you tremble, you are awake.

—KAROL WOJTYLA, 1958

The Doctors Are In

TERESA OF AVILA AND JOHN OF THE CROSS

Footsteps

A Mystical Mountain

Only events have meaning. In connection to the theory of relativity, it does not make any sense to speak about the same place tomorrow. It only makes sense to speak about events, which are combinations of the three dimensions of space. . . and a time axis.
—HOLGER B. NIELSEN, PROFESSOR, *Theoretical High Energy Physics, Niels Bohr Institute, Copenhagen*

The summer rain beat down hard upon me, high upon the hill-side. After a summer spent traveling in England, Cornwall, and South Wales, the mountains of North Wales now embla-zoned their blue-green color in my mind's eye. Not quite emerald green, the Welsh landscape is slightly bluer, like the emerald's rich cousin dioptase, and filled with teal-blue fields and forests. Drenched to the skin, I looked up the hill through my dripping hair – I was about halfway to the top.

The thunder bellowing in the churning charcoal sky made me consider turning back several times, back to the warmth and safety of nearby lodging, hearth, and pub. But I had come so far! It had to be today, this day. I had to keep going. So I continued trudging in the deluge. The higher I climbed up this mountain in Snowdonia, the more immense and overpowering the view grew, until I felt I was meeting the clouds, high above the fortress below, high above the old seaside town nestled around the harbor, up to the dead-drop cliff overlooking the Irish Sea, white waves crashing against dark rocks.

I was "walking the wave," as John Paul II advised in his poem: following a mystical calling, one that had begun in childhood, intensified through high school and college, and culminated in this adventure into my Celtic heritage. At twenty years old, I mapped out the footsteps of King Arthur – Tintagel, Caerleon, Caernarfon – and followed in his path to find my own, hoping to solve the mystery of images that both inspired and haunted me for years – images that began and ended in one simple thing: a white rose.

My journey led me here, to this place of origin, this ancient Briton site on a remote hilltop where the Celtic and Roman worlds overlapped in layers of early Christianity. And the very real white rose that had somehow called to me to find it, beckoning across time and space from a crumbling hilltop settlement to my modern Manhattan dorm room, was only a moment away –

waiting in full bloom on the mountaintop, bobbing heavily, laden with the raindrops of this summer storm. It would become the meditation piece of a lifetime. The Spirit had invited me to come and recollect this rose, a simple expression of nature's beauty somewhere in the world, and I had found it. The Grail, too, is a simple object. The gifts of mystical quests usually are.

"It is important that God doesn't lead all by one path," Teresa of Avila would write. My mystical path led me to North Wales. However, about a thousand miles due south from my Celtic flower, the country of Spain is still reaping the harvest of another spiritual rose: the journey shared by Teresa of Avila and John of the Cross, a mystical journey that would inform them, challenge them, and ultimately define their work and gift to the world.

Sometimes, the invitation to explore the mystical in life is subtle and playful. At other times, as in the case of Teresa and John, the invitation to the mystical journey arrives with our name on it, engraved, and it can shake up our world, demanding its place before all practical plans and convenience. In the end, what is more important than the prize itself is the journey of seeking it, the path that moves our gaze away from the horizon and toward the very earth on which we walk, the air we breathe, and the consciousness of our very life. The mystical journey can tap into and transform our deepest self, thereby transforming our surroundings too into heralds and manifestations of timeless symbols of love, as we will see with Teresa and John, especially in their writings. When engaging the mystical path, we connect differently with God and our own story – and the soul may unfold to full bloom.

Love Is All Around

Who can turn the world on with her smile?
Who can take a nothing day,
And suddenly make it all seem worthwhile?
Well it's you girl, and you should know it
With each glance and every little movement you show it
Love is all around, no need to waste it
You can have a town, why don't you take it
You're gonna make it after all
You're gonna make it after all

SONNY CURTIS, *"Love Is All Around,"*
The Mary Tyler Moore Show theme, 1970–1977

The year was 1970. The United States had seen a civil rights movement, a British Invasion, flower power, a summer of love, the deaths of hopeful men, Sgt. Pepper, Woodstock, anti-war protests, and now the Women's Movement. Mary Tyler Moore, the American girl next door, and the epitome of the domestic dream in *The Dick Van Dyke Show*, now sat in the driver's seat of her own prime-time television program. Her character, Mary Richards, a news producer in Minneapolis, was adored by millions and was for many (including this author) a positive role model for the single, feminine, working woman – kind, beautiful, smart, and free – living life on her own in the big city.

1970 was also the year that St. Teresa of Avila, sixteenth-century Spanish mystic, was made the first female doctor of the church by Pope Paul VI.

In many ways, Teresa was not unlike Miss Richards. Dark-haired and doe-eyed as a young woman, Teresa was attractive, vivacious, headstrong, interested in love and relationships, but ambivalent about marriage. Mary Tyler Moore, known for her charm, later said, "I was never about charm." Teresa too was charming by default, if not by intention. And her charm would be infectious, rendering her one of the most enduring writers of Christian mysticism and spirituality – one who communicated her experiences with warmth, humor, wit, candor, vulnerability, and down-to-earth humanity.

This was her gift through mysticism: to help us see that love is all around, to find the worthwhile in a nothing day, to unearth hidden symbols, to enter into a journey of self-knowledge that would lead straight to God, and then write down the directions for us.

And Teresa would "make it after all," as the song says, in life and in history. Four decades after her spiritual partner, St. John of the Cross, received the additional honor of doctor, or teacher of the universal church, Teresa of Avila joined him in this too, along with Catherine of Siena, on October 4, 1970.

John and Teresa experienced so many trials and challenges during their careers together – illness, taxing requests of superiors, the responsibility of transforming their order, the Spanish Inquisition, betrayal, a kidnapping, captivity, the challenge of founding religious houses, of being creative upon demand and under duress, of learning all manner of business and legal interactions as relating to property and real estate. The list goes on and on. At one point, Teresa, exhibiting her typical earthy sense of humor, would remark, "Lord, if this is how you treat your friends, no wonder you have so few of them."

Many of the challenges they experienced would shape and strengthen their faith, of course; in fact, Teresa and John probably considered these trials a result of their faith, a result of following the trials of Christ.

But the thing that would unlock their spiritual growth and ministry, that would give Teresa her "a-ha" moment that connected her experience of worldly friendship to her experience of God in a mature way, a way that would allow her soul to finally break free, was the wisdom gained through relationship – in this case, colleagues. The personal development of Teresa and John, as well as their ability to marry mysticism and professional skills, was propelled through relationships at work – positive, challenging, detrimental, and absolutely transformative.

THE WOMAN

Teresa Sanchez Cepeda Davila y Ahumada was born to a wealthy family in Avila, Spain, on March 28, 1515. She grew up in a nation that was at the peak of its empire, reaping material riches from the New World as well as sowing many spiritual riches at home. However, in the midst of all this strength, Teresa was a physically vulnerable child. She would be crippled by disease in her youth, and, even upon recovery, would continually battle ill health throughout her lifetime. Although her childhood illness allowed her to be privately educated at home, it also created an early pattern in Teresa's life of being set apart, of spending time alone and in her own private thoughts, reading her favorite spiritual fathers, including St. Augustine, St. Paul, and St. Gregory the Great.

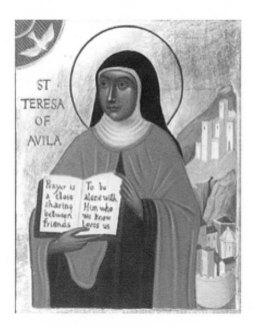

Although Teresa always was a devout Christian, I believe the most important event of Teresa's childhood, and what propelled her journey into the religious life, was the untimely death of her beautiful young mother when Teresa was fourteen. She perceived her mother as being worn down by the demands of marriage and family; this may have led to her avoidance of marriage later although she was an emerging beauty herself. In that era, there were two choices for a young woman: marriage or the convent. Her father strongly opposed her entering religious life. So, like Clare of Assisi, Teresa secretly left home one day at age seventeen and entered the Carmelite Monastery of the Incarnation in Avila, making her profession as a nun in 1535. She would become a dutiful nun, if not a passionate one. It would be another twenty years before a colleague would provide the key that unlocked the door to her spiritual freedom, igniting Teresa's ardor – and her true spiritual journey.

THE MAN

Juan de Yepes was born at Hontoveros, Old Castile, Spain, on June 24, 1542, the youngest child of Gonzalo de Yepes and Catherine Alvarez. Unlike St. Teresa, John grew up in extreme poverty in the slums of northern Spain, an area that had come to be populated by Islamic converts. John was of Arabic heritage through his mother. His father, originally from a "good" family, was perceived as marrying beneath him and was disinherited. Gonzalo and Catherine were poor silk weavers. Gonzalo died very young. John and Teresa would have this formational event in common: the loss of a beloved parent in their prime. Perhaps this is in part what inspired them as writers, the need to connect and "talk" to a departed parent whom they were able to connect to God. The treasury of romantic mystical poems that John would write as an adult would find their roots in the Moorish love ballads he grew up listening to in his neighborhood . . . the beautiful songs of his Arabic lineage.

After Gonzalo's death, Catherine sent John to the poor school at Medina del Campo, where the little tattered family had moved. There John's intellectual strengths, in addition to his faith, became apparent. The governor of the hospital of Medina invited him into his service. John worked for him for seven years, asking alms in the streets and caring for the poor, while also attending a Jesuit school. Soon John determined to enter the religious life. The Carmelite Order had a house at Medina. There John was received on February 24, 1563, and was ordained a priest in 1567. He was twenty-five.

Teresa, now in her fifties, would come to Medina to found a convent of nuns. She and John would meet, and together they would transform their order, restoring it to its original rule. They would also transform their suffering through vision; their knowledge through creativity; and their many differences through their healing union as colleagues.

SHE'S GOT PERSONALITY

Though for many years in the convent she had led a good religious life, certain faults still adhered to her . . .
    —Biography of St. Teresa of Avila, *Lives of the Saints*

The "faults" attributed to Teresa, which were no doubt gleaned in large part from her autobiographical writings and her collection of letters (she was an avid correspondent and wrote some 450 letters to various friends and colleagues) were in fact indicative of a woman in transition. The term "faults" refers to Teresa's stubbornness, her passionate, and at times volatile emotions, and what we would now call "attachments" – her investing in and commenting on people's attitudes and actions and how they affected her.

The glory of Teresa's body of work is that we get to see, to actually witness, her process of growth in spirituality, maturity, and grace. And we get to learn that, in many matters, the thoughts, concerns, and behaviors of the great saint are not unlike our own.

As a teenager, Teresa was a gregarious and flirtatious girl, experiencing the same obsessions with love and romance as any other blossoming teen. In fact, Teresa enjoyed a secret treasure with her mother during this special time: reading chivalric tales of romance and adventure. Together mother and daughter would read of love. In a romantic gesture, they would throw dried lavender onto the orange embers of the brasero, or fireplace. The lavender would fill the room with its blue smoke and sweet perfume – and Teresa's heart with intimate joy.

These heady and sensual images of sweet perfume and blue smoke also bring to mind the sweet sanctifying incense that Teresa would seek wafting through church; however, this private exquisite experience was shared with her mother Beatriz shortly before her death. And perhaps, when she died, Teresa spent many years trying to recapture that special intimacy which was so abruptly taken from her life, earmarking her personality with a pattern she would employ well into her thirties, but which she would later have to find the courage to relinquish. Teresa's need to be liked, and to be this intimate with many people, would become her core professional challenge and the pivotal point of her personal growth.

A CAFÉ SPIRITUALITY

For many years, I frequented various cafés in my hometown of New York City. Especially as a college student and throughout my twenties, it was irresistible to me to go, journal in hand, to a favorite haunt, sit ensconced by a particular window gazing on a certain view, nurse several cups of some rich brew, and write, amidst the gentle buzz of people, quiet music, conversations, and perfect anonymity in a public setting.

Of particular fondness was the Gran Caffè degli Artisti, a second-floor café overlooking Greenwich Avenue in the West Village. It was a café built in several rooms, each with a different mood, and leading to each other. First was the light and airy front room, filled with sunshine and gallery art on white walls. This led to a dark gothic room, dimly lit, with tall throne-like wooden chairs and tables with secret drawers. People who knew of them would leave notes for each other in these drawers. An enormous candle in the shape of a castle had melted down onto a fireplace mantel and was left there. A mesmerizing moonstone mirror hung on the back wall and invited the onlooker into a fairy tale. Finally, the gothic room led to a tiny "library" in the back, like a stone cell with a few shelves of books and room for only four people.

Through the 1980s and 1990s, I frequented this café often, alone or with friends, and after a long absence, with my husband and family. I cherished it like a secret nest, a private chapel. And the rooms-leading-to-rooms would become a working image for me. But sometimes we need to be careful of the things we cherish. No matter how enjoyable, they become habits and attachments, reinforcing a tendency to experience things in one way.

A DOUBLE LIFE

Teresa's convent had a parlor, or *locutorio*, a lively kind of think tank where many diverse visitors would come to discuss matters of faith with the spiritual masters in residence. Teresa became a luminary in the parlor, a theological raconteur, and she loved it. She was magnetic, accessible, and knowledgeable. She relished the attention. But she was also in a bind. Her attachment to being liked and admired, especially by men, would keep her life and work running in place for years. Teresa was a lover, a lover of people and friendship. She had a plethora of friends of both sexes, and she loved them, and loved being loved by them.

Who cannot relate to this somehow? As a freshman in college, my dormitory friends, male and female, became my closest cohorts and confidants. Our hilarious dinner conversations in the dorm dining room were almost in code – a series of puns, Monty Python gags, Bugs Bunny cartoons, and Sinatra song lyrics that only our intimate understanding of each other could interweave and understand. It was delicious. But all dinners must come to an end.

It did not end for Teresa. It was in this manner that she lived out the entire first half of her ministry. Her beloved activity of cherishing and being cherished made her feel good, but it actually kept her living a kind of double life. She was captivated by guests, captivated by her confessors, captivated by men, young and old, who appreciated her. Psychologically, she held a kind of harem in her mind, a comforting, at times exciting, massage of her ego and her worldly sense of belonging. She explains candidly in Life, her autobiography: "I had a serious fault that did me much harm; it was that when I began to know that certain persons liked me, and I found them attractive, I became so attached that my memory was bound strongly by the thought of them" (Life, 37.4).

Teresa lived this way for nearly twenty years, with one foot in the life of her professed ministry and the other foot in the world of these attachments – emotional attachments that were rooted not in her soul but in her psyche. Perhaps she relished these flirtations through her thirties because she still toyed with the idea of marriage and children. Perhaps she saw it as the possible option of a romantic life or perhaps it simply fulfilled her need to remain attractive in a sexual way. The chemistry was exhilarating, after all. But in the end she was merely distracted, and somewhere inside her the popular girl was suffering from the duality. As Teresa put it, "Neither did I enjoy God nor did I find happiness in the world. When I was experiencing the enjoyments of the world, I felt sorrow when I recalled what I owed to God. When I was with God, my attachments to the world disturbed me."

Teresa wrestled with this double life until she began to consider her distractions: Why the unease? Aren't all friendships good and desirable? Are mine in alignment with God's will for

me? Like Francis, she began to discern that, divided, she was literally wasting much of her time in a frivolous manner that nurtured one part of her personality, but not her heart, soul, or spirit. Reflecting on this, Teresa wrote in her autobiography, "One
day I was wondering if it was an attachment for me to find satisfaction in being with persons with whom I discuss my soul and
whom I love, or with those who I see are great servants of God
since it consoled me to be with them" (*Life*, 40.19).

Nothing would move forward for Teresa until she could
unravel this question. Finally she would, with the help of an honest and patient confessor who also perceived her plight, begin to
do the work of making the distinctions between the categories
above: the persons with whom she discussed her soul; the persons
whom she loved; and the great servants of God who gave her
comfort. She would begin to decipher what she meant by "satisfaction," the source of this pleasure, and her underlying motive for
seeking it.

For Teresa this was like breaking a spell. Now she could
review her life, see where she had experienced codependent
behavior with colleagues, see how many times she had fallen in
love with a priest or religious because he loved her spirit and
shared conversation about her soul, her deepest self. This was
what she valued most, and yet it was confused, all wrapped up in
a ball of romance, like her chivalric tales. Now she was able to
discern when "excessive love" occurred, or when she lost herself
or became too attached or entangled.

Once she was able to make these connections, Teresa grieved
the years wasted, realizing how she had been imprisoned by her

deeply emotional – not spiritual – needs. We can feel her all too human regret as she writes in *The Way to Perfection*, "Oh, God help me, the silly things that come from such attachments are too numerous to be counted" (*Way of Perfection*, 4.8). Then, just as openly, Teresa gives us direction on how this internal change occurred:

By turning my gaze just a little inward to behold the image I have in my soul, I obtained such freedom. . . . There is no knowledge or any kind of gift that I think could amount to anything when placed alongside of what it is to hear just one spoken word from that divine mouth.

—*Life*, 37.4

Teresa of Avila was already a spiritual master, shining as best as possible from under the bushel basket of her infatuations. Now unfettered, the master was liberated. She was about forty years old, an emotional adult. Through the help of a genuine colleague, her deeply passionate nature had been redirected and anchored – freeing her to become an honest, focused colleague as well, engaging finally in the work of her authentic self.

Her *locutorio* would now be her conversation with Spirit. Her light and airy exterior room would give way to the deeper, darker mystery of her enthroned chamber hidden within. Her mystical writings would be the notes she would leave there for others. The moonstone mirror on the back wall would become the mirror of her innermost self, at first cloudy, but now clearing and reflecting a newfound purity of intention. Finally, passing through these rooms, the private cell at the end of her journey would embrace only four people: the Holy Trinity and her.

SPIRITUAL ECSTASY

It was shortly after Teresa's self-discovery regarding her codependency and her release from empty attachments that her mystical visions began. During the years of 1556 and 1557 Teresa experienced mystical occurrences including visions and locutions. These two years of spiritual ecstasy that occurred during her early forties would direct the course of her knowledge, experience, her work reforming the Carmelites, and the writings for which she would become known.

Teresa had beautiful visions – of heaven, her parents, departed friends, the Holy Trinity, the Holy Spirit, and Jesus – but she did not trust her visions immediately and did so only with time and the encouragement of certain colleagues, including St. Peter Alcántara.

Although both Teresa and John experienced supernatural communications, visions, trances, ecstasy, and even extraordinary phenomena – for example, in her earlier experiences, Teresa would physically levitate, an event she disliked intensely and found humiliating – it is important to recall the meaning and intent of mysticism. Mysticism is the belief in the possibility of union with God by means of contemplation and self-surrender. It does not refer necessarily to supernatural gifts; rather, it focuses on accessing knowledge that is beyond the realm of the intellect, a spiritual knowledge that is encountered and engaged in chiefly symbolic terms.

While Teresa was in a state of mystical rapture, or ecstasy, her experience was marked primarily by joy, "a feeling of very great joy and sweetness" (Life, 20). However, even this joy is not the intention, or the goal, according to Teresa:

Perfection as well as its reward does not consist in spiritual delights, but in greater love and in deeds done with greater justice and truth.

—Interior Castle, 3.2.10

The fruit this extended period of mystic joy yielded was that of an advanced form of prayer for Teresa – one that grew from a sublime love.

Teresa and John's gift from mysticism would be one of union with God, in utter faith, and through all things – sweet and bitter. They would experience both.

THE DIVINE FRIEND

Prayer . . . is nothing else than an intimate sharing between friends. . . .
—TERESA OF AVILA, *Life*, 8.5

The mystical rapture Teresa experienced was rooted in prayer, and Teresa's form of prayer, like her writing, is intimate. Prayer is her connection to the Divine Friend. As a result, her relationship with God and her language of prayer is spousal. She would share this too with John: both their mystical writings express a passionate love as in the Song of Songs in the Old Testament. They speak of God as Spouse, Bridegroom, and Lover, and they speak of God in terms of embraces, physical intimacy, and, especially in the case of John, deeply private union occurring under cover of pure and mysterious night.

The way to this divine friendship is Christ. He "is the one through whom all blessings come to us." Different forms of friendship can be realized in one's relationship with Christ, Teresa reflects: He is our brother who enables us to call God our father; He is a companion, especially in times of tribulation; he is a teacher and master who teaches us how to approach God – particularly in the Our Father; he is notably in spiritual union, our Bridegroom, our Spouse; he is our Lord, the Lord of the world, our King, His Majesty. In Jesus Christ, God offers souls human friendship as well as divine.

—Classics of Western Spirituality, *Teresa of Avila: The Interior Castle*, 13

One of the reasons that Teresa and John remain so pertinent and powerful to us today is that their experience and their message remain both timely and timeless. They experienced certain challenges that were specifically of their time and place. However, they also experienced and continue to shed light on conflicts and goals that are alive and well in our contemporary society. Their human struggle to marry their spiritual passion and their work is a goal many people relate to today and strive to achieve. Many can relate to the challenge of maintaining their spiritual interests and beliefs while at the office. And, when people begin the concentrated effort of entering into a practice of prayer or meditation, many can relate to the difficult task of calming the mind amidst the noise of this busy world and the noise in our head. Teresa experienced this as well:

This intellect is so wild that it doesn't seem to be anything else than a frantic madman no one can tie down; nor am I Master of it long enough to keep it calm for the space of a creed.

—TERESA OF AVILA, *Life*, 30.16

Teresa would work with her "frantic" thoughts, learning to corral her racing mind with all its cares, concerns, and responsibilities. She did this because prayer was most important to her. Further, Teresa urged her contemporaries not to forego prayer –

spiritual nourishment – when they needed to attend to business matters or a taxing schedule. To the contrary, Teresa advised that we "shouldn't get into the habit of abandoning so great a treasure. . . . For the blessings the Lord gives in prayer are most remarkable." She adds that prayer can bring a renewed mind to business, and that "in a moment His Majesty will present to us better plans . . . than the intellect could ever search out" (Letter, 217.1).

THE CARMELITES

The Order of Our Lady of Carmel was given its rule in 1205, about the same time as the Franciscans. However, unlike the Franciscans, who created an order for women at the beginning of their movement, the admission of women into the Carmelite order would wait until the founding of a convent in the Netherlands in 1452, almost 250 years later. Other Carmelite convents would soon follow, around Europe and notably in Spain; still, it rendered Teresa of Avila a relatively new creation, a Carmelite woman. And so she would be on fire with love, brimming with enthusiasm, and met with mixed reactions.

The original Carmelite rule had its origins in desert asceticism. Now, only a few centuries later in Spain, comfort and relaxation had become the daily office. The new Carmelite convents that had sprung up, although with pious intention, came to serve basically as a home and social community for widows and unmarried women. It was not unusual for these women to continue to live the kind of life they lived before taking their vows; some lived at home, and many maintained strong ties to their families and friends.

It was only a matter of time before Teresa's intelligence, strength, and enthusiasm would land her the job of restoring the Carmelite order to its original ascetic spirit. She took on one of the largest tasks in the Spanish church at the time, inviting the young friar John of the Cross on the journey, exposing them to challenges and trials that would condemn, renew, and inspire them both.

OPPOSITES ATTRACT

St. Teresa and St. John of the Cross were friends, contemporaries and fellow workers. They were of the same Order, sharing a common purpose and . . . degree of sanctity. In almost every other aspect they were as unlike as two saints could well be.

—E. W. TRUEMAN DICKEN, *The Crucible of Love: A Study of the Mysticism of St. Teresa of Jesus and St. John of the Cross*

With Francis and Clare of Assisi we saw how two soul mates – two people so clearly alike in thought and intent and manner of living – could light up the world through their love and galvanizing expression of faith. Teresa of Avila and John of the Cross would also set the spiritual world on fire, but they were so completely different in so many ways, we might consider them a veritable model of the Jungian complements anima and animus, yin and yang, the paradoxical union of opposites. Science tells us that when it comes to matter, or substance, like attracts like. But when it comes to magnetism, or electricity, opposites attract.

She was an older woman, he a younger man.
Yet he called her daughter; she called him father.
She was of Jewish heritage; he, Arabic.

She came from affluence. He came from poverty.
Yet he was formally educated; she was not.

His writing is refined, elegant, and scholarly.
Her writing is rustic, straightforward, and vernacular.

He writes in broad impersonal terms.
She writes from deep personal experience.

John was not known for any administrative ability and was not given assignments involving organizational skills or negotiations.
Teresa was an effective negotiator and worldly administrator.

John was a model of self-control and self-discipline.
Teresa was motherly and doting, often seeking assurance and comfort.

John would master detachment from the material things of this world that entrap.
Teresa would master detachment from personal ties that bind.

They were both obedient.

There is a robust heartiness, even a masculine boldness, about Teresa's character, which creates much of her motivational quality. John is visionary and inspired by beauty. In this way we begin to see how Teresa embodies many traits of the animus at work, the masculine qualities often associated with strength, penetration, and outward expression of passion; and John, the anima, or the feminine qualities often associated with the inner workings of life, creation, mystery, and pure spirit.

I believe our Lord has called [John] to this task. There's not a friar who does not speak well of him, for he had been living a life of great penance, even though he is young. It seems the Lord is watching over him carefully, for although in trying to get everything settled we met with a number of troubles – and I myself must have caused trouble at times by becoming annoyed with him – we never saw an imperfection in him.

  —TERESA OF AVILA writing about John, Letter 13.2

Teresa believed that John of the Cross was always a saint, and referred to his saintliness in her correspondence (Letters 48.2, 51.1), usually adding others' supporting witness of John's holiness. However, when they worked together as colleagues she found qualities in him that "annoyed" her, and her correspondence indicates that she made her annoyance known, perhaps adding another layer of difficulty to the situation.

Teresa's annoyance most likely emerged from simple differences in personality type. Teresa was a gifted manager, and John had little to no capacity for administration whatsoever. We can see how this complement might vex in the founding and building of facilities, even spiritual ones. But we also see something highly notable in Teresa: Although she experienced traits in John that disappointed and angered her, she was able to separate them from his character, continuing to perceive him without imperfection. This is a mature attitude toward colleagues – to recognize gifts, abilities, and limitations, without judgment of the person as "good" or "bad." When we are not able to make this distinction, the human beings we work with may be reduced to mere "obstacles" in our path, thus diminishing our experience of work, productivity, and our own personhood.

Instead, Teresa and John developed a system based on their skills: Teresa would found the institutions, handling real estate, legal matters, construction, and financial procurement. Then she turned over the responsibility of spiritual formation of the friars to John. They were both supreme architects – Teresa, the external architect, and John, the interior.

In this way, Teresa and John, with their myriad of opposite skills and qualities, formed a complete wholeness of talent, filled the gaps and wanting places in each other, and with a singleness of effort moved their entire community of colleagues forward.

TAKE OFF YOUR SANDALS

Like Francis of Assisi, Teresa was asked to rebuild God's house. But unlike the crumbling structure of San Damiano that Francis rebuilt stone by stone, what she would rebuild with John's help was internal and personal. What they would rebuild was the Carmelite community, proud people and their way of life. The challenges would be formidable and often painful. Resisting change and the unknown, their fellow Carmelites would fight Teresa and John bitterly.

Teresa's mystical visions had already prompted her to found St. Joseph Convent in Avila, according to the ascetic vision of the order's original rule. For this she was met with ridicule and opposition from colleagues who had taken advantage of the relaxed rule for so long. But she had created a prototype. Now, in 1567, the Prior General of the Carmelites, Father Rubeo, gave Teresa permission to establish other convents in the same tradition as St. Joseph's.

Teresa's reform was in part a turning away from affluence, in part a return to prayer and contemplation, to austerity and the road toward mystical union. She was founding small convents and monasteries throughout Spain, and also arousing intense enmity among the unreformed Carmelites.

—WILLIS BARNSTONE, *The Poems of Saint John of the Cross*

What arose from this motion toward change is famous: a bitter struggle with the Calced (meaning "sandaled") Carmelites, who feared their easy-going lifestyle would be threatened by this new wave of renewed asceticism that was being forged by "the roving nun" and her spiritual accomplice John of the Cross. Teresa recalls when she first met John at Medina:

While I was there, I was always thinking over the monasteries of friars; and since, as I said, I had not one friar, I did not know what to do . . . . A little while later, there happened to come a young Father who had been studying at Salamanca. Another priest accompanied him, who told me great things of the life that this Father lived. His name was Brother John of the Cross. I gave thanks to our Lord. When I talked to the Father, I was much pleased with him. He told me he meant to become a Carthusian. I told him my projects, and earnestly begged him to wait until the Lord should give us a monastery, pointing out that if he meant to better himself, it would be a great gain to do so within his own Order. . . . He gave me his word that he would, if he had not to wait too long.

—TERESA OF AVILA, *Foundations*, 3

With John's help, Teresa founded the first monastery for men under the Discalced (meaning "without sandals," or "unshod") rule – the return to the original ascetic spirit of the order – and continued to travel throughout Spain establishing forty such communities in her lifetime.

The unreformed Carmelites met John with constant harass-
ment, threats, and struggle for control, all of which contributed to
the fears and emptiness he felt and wrote about in his classic work
Dark Night of the Soul. Finally, in 1580 Pope Gregory XIII, with the
urging of the king of Spain, Philip II, officially recognized the two
distinct Carmelite branches – Calced and Discalced. The Pope's
action protected the Discalced from those who sought to damage
the reputations of Teresa and John. However, this did not prevent
the suffering that John was yet to endure.

THE CROSS

When John first entered his Carmelite community, he initially
took the name John of St. Matthew. As his commitment deepened,
he took the name John of the Cross. Why the change? Perhaps, as
Saul of Tarsus became St. Paul, John believed that the real work of
God was beginning in his life. Or, perhaps the change in name –
like the bride in his poetry – marked the changed identity of this
new consummation with God. Or, perhaps the change in name
was a premonition or call for protection, for John's ministry would
become even more difficult than it had already been, and he would
imitate Christ to the end, by the humiliation, abandonment, and
physical suffering he would endure.

What began as a mystical vision for Teresa became an issue of
corporate identity change and management among the Carmelites,
and finally a devastating political nightmare for John.

On the night of December 3, 1577, a gang broke into the
house where John was living, and he was taken prisoner to the
Carmelite Priory in Toledo. Here accounts vary. Some say his

colleagues kept him in a dark cupboard-like cell not tall enough for him to stand in. Others say that he was held in a guesthouse latrine and that the constant stench month after month made him very ill. He was fed bread, water, and sardine scraps on the floor. Treated like the worst kind of criminal, he was beaten by monks with leather whips until his shoulders were permanently maimed. He was not allowed changes of clothing. He became infested with lice and had dysentery.

In August of 1578, he determined to escape somehow. After having a dream in which the Virgin Mary promised to assist him, he was resolved to get away. Around 2 A.M. he pried loose the hinges of his cell and lowered himself down from a balcony, using as a rope pieces of his own clothing and blankets tied together. He jumped down into a courtyard that was enclosed by high walls. In his sick and fragile state he managed to climb over those walls, undetected; this is where Mary helped him, he said. Suddenly, after so many months of captivity and neglect, John stood on a dark street in Toledo, a free man.

He first took refuge in a convent of Discalced Carmelites, and then in a small hermitage in El Calvario, where he wrote most of his poetry, a period of creativity, recovery, and joy reborn from this terrible life-threatening occurrence.

His freedom would not last long, however. After Teresa's death, John engaged again in one more political battle: supporting the rights of the nuns in the Madrid convent to use the secret ballot to elect their new prioress. He hoped that the nuns would be able to vote and govern themselves democratically. Then a false rumor began to spread of a romantic relationship between John and a nun at the convent. For this, he was stripped of all authority and responsibility and was completely ostracized, a heretic. Sadly, even his letters were burned. It is believed that John would have been expelled from his own order, if he had not become ill:

There was a move to expel him from the order, and only his sickness spared him this last step. Suffering from fever and ulcers on the legs, he went to nearby Ubeda for treatment. But the Prior refused to give him the barest necessities and treated him with vengeful hostility, coming each day to his cell to insult him. The ulcers spread. His body was literally rotting away.

—WILLIS BARNSTONE, *The Poems of Saint John of the Cross*

There is an account that John apologized to the prior on December 13, 1591, for the difficulties he had caused, and that the prior apologized as well and left John's cell in tears; however, this reconciliation did not negate the abuse and neglect that John suffered. He died the following day, December 14, 1591.

THE ORGANIZATIONAL CHART

Of course, it does not happen often that a bitter feud among colleagues results in this kind of extreme cruelty and persecution, even unto death; nonetheless, there remain corporate patterns that Teresa and John encountered that we may see glimpses of in our own lives.

Teresa and John were sublime mystics and great spiritual guides. But look at that in light of their "job" in their "company."

If we created an "org chart" of the Carmelites, we might see that Teresa and John were middle management, not CEOs. As managers, they were entrusted with a project – ambitious, but doable – one of spearheading great change throughout the company. It was a goal set from the top, carried out by the middle, and expected to take root with everyone else. Unfortunately, things did not go as planned.

First, the project did not begin from the bottom; that is, it did not rise up or come out of the needs expressed by the company at large, nor was a plan shared or approved. It was imposed on them. Therefore, Teresa and John were placed in a vulnerable position among their own. Some welcomed them as heroes; others condemned them as traitors.

One result was typical: when met with tremendous hostility, superiors scaled back the efforts of Teresa and John. They were "reeled back in," so to speak, showing a lapse of support and also a kind of punitive response to the problem. The discord was not the fault of Teresa and John; they did nothing wrong and were merely carrying out orders in obedience, with the highest of hopes and the best of intentions.

Further, senior management tried to handle the problem at its bitter end by officially creating two branches of the company. This may have been an attempt to stanch the bleeding of a warring structure, but it came too late and could not address the venomous emotions that had built up over time. The company would have to heal from what was no less than a civil war.

"It is only in uncertainty that we are naked and alive," sang British pop star Peter Gabriel, naked and alive to our real selves in our real environment. Uncertainty – call it a place of all possibilities and no known outcomes – is a matrix from which our truest desires may emerge to be named and made manifest. Uncertainty is also the favored hiding place of our nay-saying gremlins, known and unknown, that may hinder us from achieving fullness of life.

The way we react to change, as individuals or as a company, will say a lot about the amount of suffering we encounter in life. The Carmelite order suffered greatly during this time of upheaval. The changes were painful, and one might say the "messengers were shot."

But what of Teresa and John? Through all this, they maintained their focus. They learned not to be swayed by what others thought and said. They ignored gossip. Concerning this, Teresa wrote:

There was a great deal of talk. Some said I was mad; others would wait to see the end of this nonsense. To the Bishop, as I was afterwards told, it seemed great folly, although at the time he did not let me know this, because, having a great affection for me, he did not like to hamper me or cause me pain. My friends gave me their opinion roundly; but I attached little weight to it; because to me that which they thought hazardous seemed so easy that I could not persuade myself that it could fail to turn out well.

—TERESA OF AVILA, *Foundations*, 3.3

They held the eternal in mind and fixed their gaze on God, who, Teresa says, "never takes His eyes off you." And they continued in their own private endeavors and works, utilizing and nurturing their unique gifts.

TERESA'S TEACHINGS

The soul . . . does not move from that center nor is its peace lost; for the very One who gave peace to the apostles when they were together can give it to the soul.

—TERESA OF AVILA, *The Interior Castle: The Seventh Dwelling Place, 6*

Both Teresa and John wrote great literary masterpieces during times of duress. Teresa's writing career would take place in the last twenty years of her life, and she often wrote in response to the demand of superiors and confessors who wished to learn more of her unusual and mystical journey, as well as how God moved through her life. In contrast to John's refined, meticulous language, Teresa's work is more of an unedited stream of consciousness; she rarely used punctuation, and much of her meaning is gleaned through context. Her style is chatty, straightforward, warm, and in the vernacular of her day.

Life, her autobiography, was completed in 1565 and documents the pivotal and memorable events of her childhood and adolescence, detailing her religious call and journey, her struggles and graces, including her mystical path and a treatise on prayer.

The Way of Perfection, which explains the necessity and practice of the reformed Carmelite rule, was intended for her sisters. It was written about the same time as her autobiography, but it was not finalized until 1569 after edits by censors. This book of teachings focuses on a life of unceasing prayer.

Foundations, written during the last year of her life, chronicles the arduous journey with John to found the reformed convents and monasteries. It also demonstrates how her inner life informs and guides her work.

The Mansions, or *The Interior Castle,* is probably Teresa's greatest and best-known work. Written in just a few months at the peak of the troubled Carmelite reform, it is Teresa's allegorical description of the soul's journey to God through ever-increasing levels of prayer, represented by passing through the rooms of a crystal castle to its center.

Like a labyrinth, the outermost rooms give access inwardly to the next series of rooms, and so on. The soul must journey through these different rooms (challenges) and levels (of prayer) to get to the innermost chamber of the crystal castle, the Seventh Dwelling, which represents the achievement of spiritual union with God. There resides the source of the crystal's radiant Light, the King on his throne. In an uncertain world, Teresa draws strength and comfort from the image of this steadfast and ever-present sovereign that represents the soul in its rightful place:

The King is in His palace and there are many wars in his kingdom and many painful things going on, but not on that account does he fail to be at his post.

—*The Interior Castle: The Seventh Dwelling Place,* 11

THE LEGACY OF JOHN

I did not know the door
But when I found the way,
Unknowing where I was,
I learned enormous things,
But what I felt I cannot say,
For I remained unknowing,
Rising beyond all science.

—JOHN OF THE CROSS, "*I Came Into the Unknown,*"

Like the white lotus blossom growing purely in the mud, John's soul bloomed, reaching up from the dark and murky terrain of hatred and despair, to the warm and guiding light that always penetrated and illumined his darkness, a light he never questioned and that never failed.

The most beautiful poems he left us emerged from the most dark and dangerous time of his life, his imprisonment. We know of eleven central poems, although there may have been more. John, with his self-effacing personality, simply may not have seen the importance of holding on to them. Also, given his singleness of purpose, he may have destroyed others along with personal letters from Teresa for their own protection during the persecution of their reform. To John, the protection and nurturing of their work would have been more important to preserve than any poetic reflection, no matter how great or masterful.

The paradoxes – union through opposites – explored earlier about John and Teresa's personalities continue in John's work as a poet. He is a writer of paradox. He sifts the darkness to find light, and when he finds it, he is stunned by its brightness. He finds life in death, union in solitude, higher knowledge in perpetual unknowing.

The higher he ascends
The darker is the wood;
It is the shadowy cloud
That clarified the light,
And so the one who understood
Remains always unknowing,
Rising beyond all science.

—JOHN OF THE CROSS, "I Came Into the Unknown"

Following his time of imprisonment, John went deeper into faith, with generosity of spirit and no evidence of rancor or resentment regarding his circumstances. To the contrary; he is a man with nothing left who surrenders his very being to God:

I gave my soul to him
And all the things I owned were his:
I have no flock to tend
Or any other trade
And my one ministry is love.

— JOHN OF THE CROSS, "Spiritual Canticle"

And, capturing the mystery of faith, life, and love, culminating in the gift of communion, is John's poem "The Fountain," which I include here in its entirety:

How well I know that flowing spring
in black of night.

The eternal fountain is unseen.
How well I know where she has been
    in black of night.
I do not know her origin.
None. Yet in her all things begin
    in black of night.
I know that nothing is so fair
And earth and firmament drink there
    in black of night.
I know that none can wade inside
To find her bright bottomless tide
    in black of night.
Her shining never has a blur;
I know that all light comes from her
    in black of night.
I know her streams converge and swell
And nourish people, skies and hell
    in black of night.
The stream whose birth is in this source
I know has a gigantic force
    in black of night.
The stream from but these two proceeds
Yet neither one, I know precedes
    in black of night.
The eternal fountain is unseen
In living bread that gives us being
    in black of night.
She calls on all mankind to start

To drink her water, though in dark,
*   for black is night.*
O living fountain that I crave,
In bread of life I see her flame
*   in black of night.*

—JOHN OF THE CROSS, "The Fountain"

Teresa and John were able to work, to love, and to be profoundly creative, through all manner of challenge, obstacle, illness, and even persecution. Their literary work rose from the center of their soul and continues to call to the core of human spiritual experience across time.

They were able to do this because they kept God at the center – the center of their work, their vision, their relationships, their joy, and their sorrow. With God at the beginning and the end of all their hopes, goals, and endeavors, Teresa and John were able to take personal conflicts and limitations in stride and overcome much larger obstacles with grace. Their lives are a testimony to character, resilience, and ineffable imagination at work, but above all, to love that does not fail.

Please God the work will be done well, and may he keep you,
as I beg him, for his service, amen.

—TERESA OF AVILA, Letter 185.13, February 28, 1577

Love Notes

What We Can Learn from Teresa and John

Attachments

When engaging in the work of our calling, in any career, aspects of our personality – the temporal part of us that learned certain traits to interact with the world – can hold us back from progress. As we explored in this chapter, people, places, and even the methods we employ to accomplish tasks may become attachments. Explore your life in terms of attachment, excessive love, or misplaced love, perhaps romanticizing people who were put in your life for other reasons. Were there missed (or misinterpreted) opportunities? Don't grieve too much; celebrate the maturity you continue to gain in life. Think of a habit or activity you really enjoy. Is it good for you, promoting growth? If not, can it be replaced? These "tweaks" may be difficult, but the results are well worth it.

Popularity

Pope Paul VI, the man who pronounced Teresa a doctor of the church, attempted to live closer to the gospel life than other popes amidst the Vatican's splendor (he sold his coronation crown to give the money to the poor). However, he was not popular like his predecessor Pope John XXIII. In fact, John XXIII once commented that Paul's personality was "a little like Hamlet's."

What is the importance of personality?

Is it important to be a 'popular' pope?

Is it important that any leader live up to the popularity of his or her predecessor?

Or does that merely impose another layer of concerns to contend with?

Popularity has been the spiritual death of many a good priest. A minister's need to be liked has provided good punch lines on a variety of contemporary issues and pursuits, while killing the impact of more sermons than I could count. Speaking one's truth directly may repel some people, but it will also attract others whose spiritual needs do not require sugar coating. For example:

A small Episcopal parish outside of New York City went through a change in leadership. The new priest, a middle-aged woman with a recent doctorate, gave her first sermon, a hard-hitting social commentary about Holy Week. After mass, she shook everyone's hand as they emerged from church. A well-dressed elderly woman spoke up.

"This used to be such a charming little church," she said, "with a charming priest, who gave such charming homilies."

The new priest leaned closer to the woman and replied, "Remember – this charming little church began with a charming little crucifixion."

Somewhere along the way, we all learn that what is good for us is not necessarily what we want to hear.

Conflicts

During the course of our career, we may find ourselves in a position in which we do not get along with a superior, an important colleague, or even an assistant assigned to help us. Or there may be intense competition at the office, which we do not share and which frightens us – a very real and common concern. Will I be able to keep my job in this atmosphere? Or there may be a frustrating lack of clear communication or clear procedures. These challenges can rob us of our joy at work if we are not able to discern an authentic way to engage.

We can always change jobs, yes, but chances are that some conflict will arise there too. It's the nature of the beast – even when we work for ourselves. Often, some less pleasing aspects of work can be changed and improved with the right attitude; others may never evolve. Nonetheless, most of us work, remain dedicated, and do not want to walk away from our commitments. Still, it is very important to find peace and meaning in what we do with our lives every day.

From Teresa and John we learn that no matter how different people can be, our complements just may add up to a perfect whole for the task at hand. Humility does not only refer to the modest knowing of ourselves and the things we cannot do; if Teresa and John had stopped there, they would have accomplished nothing. Humility also means knowing the things we can do, and stepping up to it, in community.

Opposites

Explore how opposite traits and qualities have been at work in
your relationships (and perhaps even in yourself): love relationships, friendships, work and club relationships. Consider a relationship that works well and why; a smile may come to your face.
Consider also where there have been tensions, conflicts, or dissat-
isfaction. This too will generate an immediate inner response.
How could these interactions be assisted by detachment and a
renewed imagination? Try thinking in terms of what is complementary rather than contradictory between you and a person with
whom you experience tension. Speak to someone you trust about
this, and/or reflect on it in your journal.

Mysticism

Today both St. Teresa and St. John of the Cross are known primarily as mystics. Their experiences and writings are famous, and
have set an example of mysticism and how it can be lived out,
informing daily life and work, and vice versa. As in Teresa's era,
many find it fashionable today to seek out mystical texts and experiences, perhaps as an alternative to confining dogma and doctrine,
and also as a pathway and indication of growth. Yet Teresa and
John tell us themselves that the soul's sanctity and the ultimate
value of a person's spiritual life are, strictly speaking, not connected with or dependent upon mystical experiences. Further, Teresa
was strongly vigilant about false mystical experiences, thoroughly
discerning her own as well. Today, with such emphasis and import
placed upon spiritual leaders, and our ability to follow people
claiming to "have all the answers," it is easy to see how we may

become misled regarding their purpose and their role. Teresa and John consistently pointed to God, our origin and destiny.

Inner Life

We all have an inner life, inner thoughts, and inner voice, whether or not we believe in God or have a spiritual path. We also tend to seek wholeness in our life and to eliminate incongruities and dualities, for a variety of reasons. Those who do believe in a spiritual source of their inner life tend to want to unite their interior and exterior lives as much as possible as an authentic expression of love. Consider your inner life (your dreams, hopes, passions, beliefs, vision, and longings). Does your inner life have a forum in which to emerge? A great way to honor and reveal our inner life is by keeping a journal. Doing so even for a few minutes each day will unveil our inner life, which speaks in its own unique voice, one you will come to recognize as a form of prayer or union.

❖

We must go below the marble floor,
with its generations of footsteps,
and drill through the rock to find the man
trampled by hooves of sheep.
They knew not whom they trampled – a passing man?
the Man who never will pass?
The crypt speaks: I am bound to the world and besieged;
the world is an army of exhausted soldiers
who will not pull back.
—KAROL WOJTYLA, "The Crypt"

Peacemakers of Metropolis

CATHERINE OF SIENA AND POPE GREGORY XI

Footsteps

Trump Tower

Christmas Eve, Manhattan, 1988. I emerge from the apartment of a colleague hosting a holiday party with a Charles
Dickens theme. After reading from *A Christmas Carol* and imbibing
a hot holiday punch, I step outside onto a snowy silent street on
the east side, a street where I can still see the remnants of the
bygone Victorian era in the architecture – especially tonight, a
quiet, carless night.

I pull up my wool collar around my neck and begin my walk
toward the Fifth Avenue train station. On one of the street cor-
ners a grocery store is still open, with a display of Christmas bou-
quets outside in the falling snow. There are red roses, pink, white
– my white roses – wrapped for Christmas with evergreen and

holiday ribbon. They still speak to me, five years after the mountain in North Wales. I buy the white roses and continue toward
the train.

Along the way are some of the most affluent properties in the
city, perhaps the world. Still in my mid-twenties, I don't have
very much – I have no life partner or child or country getaway, but
I do have a sweet apartment, a good job, and loving friends. And
so I feel rich and grateful, in the way that city girls do, with my
whole life ahead of me sparkling in the new snow.

I cross Madison Avenue, still heading west, and begin the
walk alongside Trump Tower. On the Madison Avenue side of
the building is something wonderful – a huge glass atrium with a
bamboo garden inside, an excellent place to take a break, to have

lunch, or to meet a friend. Tonight it is open, a shelter to the homeless. As I walk, I look through the tremendous glass windows and see all kinds of people resting on the benches, having something to eat, clinging together on Christmas Eve. I see four homeless people, one woman and three men, sitting around a table playing cards among deli cups of coffee and old stained parkas. The woman is in her late forties, brown hair streaked with grey. I am walking past the entrance door . . . and I slow down.

I turn around and open the door. Entering the garden, I walk to the woman. Gently I hand her my bouquet of roses and say "Merry Christmas." She takes them and stares at the ivory velvet blossoms, speechless. Finally a gentleman friend speaks for her, putting down his cards.

"You couldn't have given them to a nicer girl." We smile.

And so the anonymous woman helps me to understand that the gift of finding the white rose is to give it away, not to hold it, striving instead to become the rose itself.

And there is no better place to give away the sacred than Metropolis, a place where strangers cross barriers and boundaries each day, stepping out of life and character to greet each other on alternative, merciful, and sometimes exalted planes of existence.

Every city enjoys its own mythology, identity, and even nickname; and each phrase conjures in our mind an image unique to the place, its energy, its environment and aspirations: Rome is the Eternal City; Paris, the City of Light. Cairo is Mother of the World. Hong Kong is the Pearl of the Orient. Venice is Bride of the Sea. Mexico City was known as the City of Palaces, which was changed in 2000 to the City of Hope. Madurai, India, is called the Athens of the East; Berkeley, California, the Athens of the West. Edinburgh, Scotland, is affectionately nicknamed Auld Reekie, or Old Smoky. São Paulo is Brazil's Locomotive. Calgary, Alberta is the Heart of the New West. Montreal is the Bell Tower and the City of Saints. Århus, Denmark, is the City of Smiles. Munich, Germany, is the World City with Heart. Tel Aviv is the City That Never Stops. New York is the City That Never Sleeps. Oxford, England, is the City of Dreaming Spires.

After leaving Trump Tower, I walk a little further down Fifth Avenue and arrive at the magnificent promenade of herald angels at Rockefeller Plaza. They lead to a magical, towering Christmas tree known the world over. And there, beneath the tree, overlooking the skating rink, is a golden statue of Prometheus. Captured at the moment of victory and joy, he raises his right hand and shows us the fire he has stolen from the gods, from the wheel of Apollo's chariot, the heavenly fire he has brought to humanity regardless of personal risk. Behind him is engraved the description of Prometheus as "teacher," and he very much remains a powerful symbol of all who have journeyed to the Big Apple to seize some part of universal greatness, the mysterious cosmic fire, come what may.

"My nature is fire," said Catherine of Siena.

The story of Catherine of Siena and Pope Gregory XI is a story of cities and city people, people who, with each step, sense both the ancient and newborn markings of humanity. The great urban center is one of balance by paradox – a balance between harmony and cacophony; between the man-made and the natural; between solitude and crowding closeness; between the accomplishment of daily life and the larger vision that continues to inspire it; between what is temporal and passing and what is timeless and eternal.

The city offers all and challenges all. It is only as strong as its infrastructure, yet its dreaming spires reach for the heavens. Catherine and Gregory would reach for the heavens too, bringing their special fire to the arena of faith, helping to heal the many layers of humanity in their capital, from children in the streets to the church at large, the mighty and powerful in their towers.

THE WOMAN

She was the daughter of Zeus alone. [Born] full-grown and in full armor . . . She was pre-eminently the Goddess of the City, the protector of civilized life, of handicrafts and agriculture; the inventor of the bridle, who first tamed horses for men to use. The word oftenest used to describe her is "gray-eyed," or, as it is sometimes translated, "flashing-eyed." She was Zeus's favorite child. He trusted [only] her to carry the awful aegis . . . and his devastating weapon, the thunderbolt.

—EDITH HAMILTON, *on the goddess Athena,* Mythology, 29

She was born Catarina di Benincasa in Siena, Italy, on March 25, 1347, the twenty-fourth child of an extensive family of twenty-five. Her father, Giacomo, was a dyer, and her mother, Lapa, was a poet's daughter. They belonged to the "Party of the Twelve," a lower middle class alliance of tradesmen that governed Siena from 1355 to 1368. And so, from an early age, Catherine was politically aware and attuned to the challenges and suffering of her surrounding society in the city – the Black Plague, civil wars, economic struggle, and poverty – and was drawn to God and to helping her neighbors through love. The budding protectoress consecrated herself to God at the tender age of seven.

During her childhood, the Franciscan and Dominican communities would take root and flourish in busy urban centers like Siena; and these communities' growth made sense, as their refreshing spirituality offered a simpler way of life, raising up and celebrating the sacred in the everyday, and offering people a way to find context and meaning – something many city dwellers seek to this day.

As Catherine grew, she was spiritually directed by the Dominicans and took the habit as a Dominican sister at the age of sixteen. Focused and driven far beyond her years, she was gifted, passionate, and eager to be of service, especially to the poor, the sick, and the condemned. There is a stunning story of her courage, standing beside a man at his execution. They prayed together, Catherine stroking his head on the block, until his head fell into her hands.

Catherine's faith, compassion, and courage began to attract a family of devout followers, including her confessor and biographer, Fra Raimondo delle Vigne of Capua, who would become General of the Dominicans, and Stefano di Corrado Maconi, one of the people who would aid Catherine as a secretary, and who would later become Prior General of the Carthusians.

As her career progressed, Catherine would serve in an increasingly public way, entering into correspondence with people of all walks of life, including the warring princes and republics of Italy – calling them to conversion and to peace.

THE MAN

Pope Gregory XI was born Pierre Roger de Beaufort in 1331 at the castle of Maumont in Limoges, France. He was the nephew of Pope Clement VI. Like Catherine, his family and environment inspired his calling and work at a tender age. He was still a teenager, only nineteen, when his uncle made him cardinal. As cardinal, he attended the University of Perugia, where he became a skilled canonist and theologian.

In an extraordinary rite of passage, Pierre was elected pope in December 1370, although he was not yet a priest. The following month, he was ordained as priest and was crowned Pope Gregory XI the next day, January 5, 1371. He was forty years old.

Gregory was a good and honest man living in a time of great conflict and corruption. He was known for his intelligence, generosity, and upstanding character. He supported religious endeavors and religious reform, something he would share with Catherine. Above all, he was a peacemaker who desired and worked to reconcile the places of unrest in his time, including Castile, Aragon, Navarre, Sicily, and Naples; the warring kings of France and England; and even the historic rift between the Greek and Latin churches. And so in Gregory we begin to see the pattern of working to heal, to bring together that which has been divided, and the courage to approach even the largest of schisms with continued belief and vision.

This desire and work would be the cornerstone of his papacy, culminating in a conflict with the city of Florence in which Catherine would become his adviser, sage, and ambassador – a young Merlin to his Arthur.

Homecoming:
Their Great Task

Catherine and Gregory lived during the time of the Avignon popes, a period when the French papacy had retreated from Rome to France for the better part of the fourteenth century. Until that point, the Holy See had always been in Rome; and so this jarring absence was a time of escalating tensions, of scornful confrontations between Italian city-states and French authority, of corruption among church officials. A great feud between the city of Florence and the Holy See culminated in the temporary excommunication of Florence, a tremendous shock to that city both religiously and economically that provoked nearly all papal states to rise in insurrection. War broke out. These were developments that, unchecked, could lead to the bitterest suffering and the kind of damage that could devastate the church.

Although he was surrounded by corruption, Gregory himself remained a man of principle. He loved his French birthplace dearly, and he loved his family, who had begged him (literally on hands and knees) to stay in France; they had become a veritable court of popes handing down the coronation through generations like royalty. But Gregory remained a man of principle. His commitment to the church and the greater good made him act on his conscience, deciding to restore the seat of papal authority to Rome. He would be the last Avignon pope. But he did not make this transition alone.

As was often the custom in the medieval period, Gregory was drawn to seek advice from reputed holy people and mystics in his planning and decision making. First to act as his guide was St. Brigit of Sweden. Her messages for Gregory emphasized two things: Rome and peace. When Brigit died in 1373, Gregory sought out Catherine, whose reputation for holiness and action was growing like wildfire. When Catherine's guidance offered a reprise of the same themes, Rome and peace, he found the sure signposts of the right path and bolstered his will for what lay ahead. In addition, her fearlessness and fiery words fueled his courage and determination.

Catherine's initial contact with Gregory was made in March of 1374, fours years into his papacy. Their exchanges would range over a variety of issues, but overarching these was their common desire for peace in Italy, the reform of clergy, and the return of the papal seat to Rome.

What can we discern from Catherine's written responses to his messages? That Gregory often requested her prayers; sought her advice about the timing of his return to Rome; and, like his guardian angel, asked her predictions regarding his physical safe-ty during and after the journey from France. He continued contact with her until his return to Rome. But he would hear a great deal more than that from Catherine.

THE AUTHENTIC SELF

Catherine's and Gregory's lives, work, and relationship are marked by the mature spirituality of the authentic self. Authenticity – self-actualization, maturity, integration, fulfill-ment, inner peace, vitality, whatever we want to call it – is some-thing we strive for either consciously or subconsciously in life, knowing from our internal barometer whether or not we are headed in the right direction during the limited amount of time we have here on this earth. But as we asked before, what does actualized divine love look like? How does the authentic self flourish? What are the characteristics of spiritual maturity? Let us observe some outward traits of Catherine and Gregory, and then explore more deeply the source of these traits, how they worked in their lives, and how they can work in ours.

Many of us tend to spend years discerning the details of our life and the direction it will take – how our life will be spent, with what line of work, where, and why. As young people we cannot wait to grow up, imitating adults and aspiring to a romantic future persona we do not yet embody. Then, when we are adults, and faced with the passing years, it seems that there just isn't enough time to be exactly who we are! And so authenticity becomes deeply important to us. The person we are – the spirit, the personality, the body – is precious and unique; now we realize it always has been.

In Catherine's case, one quality of maturity was her ability not to waste time. Although she was young, her faith was mature and her feet were planted on the ground. She did not have to look very far to find her life. She just had to look around her. There was much work to be done, and she approached it without fear. One of her biographers describes the passionate young woman as one who was always going "at full tilt." Catherine knew herself and what motivated her. She did not take years out of what would be a short life to search for the right thing to do. She put her trust in God and acted on what was placed before her.

Although Catherine was illiterate for a good deal of her life, she did not let this keep her from self-expression. Undaunted by her limitations, she dictated her literary masterpieces, sometimes reciting three different pieces to three scribes simultaneously. Eventually, she would teach herself to read and to write as well. In the end she would leave behind her legacy *The Dialogue* and nearly four hundred letters to a wide-ranging cross section of people throughout society. Centered in God, Catherine believed in the validity and authority of her thoughts and words, regardless of the lack of a formal education, credentials, or titles. Her faith was her credential. She required no further permission or approval.

Catherine believed that the kingdom of God lies within each and every one of us. This was the most important message she wished to convey, and the underlying belief that drove her actions and words. We come from joy, from God's love and grace, and his mercy and peace rest within each of us. This is what propelled Catherine's challenging letters to so many readers in her day: she shocked them into recollection, into recalling their true nature, which they had forgotten or lulled to sleep somehow in their worldly offices, conflicts, desires, and illusions.

Also with her maturity comes a timelessness about her understanding of her world and faith, which is why she remains pertinent to us today. With Catherine we share the uncertain world. We can be shocked by developments in our world. Just as we stared at the fallout of 9-11, Catherine, from her perch in her city, witnessed much change and upheaval all about her: war, plague, corruption, economic and religious conflict, and even galvanizing changes in technology (her era would see the printing press revolutionize literacy, religion, and access to education). Catherine managed to distill the clarity through all the confusion of her day, and was able to draw it out for others as well.

In Gregory, we saw someone who lived according to his conscience, whether or not his actions earned him approval or popularity. He was concerned with the right thing to do; and the right thing was not necessarily the prettiest or easiest route. He was not concerned so much with how he appeared, or how historians would remember him, as he was with the work at hand.

He also knew himself, and accepted that, as a corporate leader, he had a mystical side, one that sought out another's opinion from a different, broader, more celestial point of view. He required that point of view as he faced his major tasks and decisions. This was how Gregory came to engage Catherine in his life; they both engaged the present with an eye to the eternal. He initiated contact, seeking her thoughts as a mystic on the many challenges they both witnessed taking place in their church, cities, and country.

For Catherine, peace began with the individual. From this beginning place, peace is possible with those around us – our family, our neighbors, and our own spiritual fellowship. Then, like ripples expanding on the surface of a lake, peace can reach out to the extended community, to other towns, cities, and peoples. But it "begins at home," as the adage goes. And often that is the difficult place to begin.

In my experience of religious peace work, I have seen numerous examples of how easy, even fashionable, it is for us to offer the hand of peace to people of other religions and cultures. It is exciting and attractive to gather Christians, Jews, Muslims, and Buddhists, for example, across religious lines in an act of peace. It is far more difficult to unite the various sects and denominations within one of these religions; that is, to reconcile differing siblings of the same faith. Sharing an experience of communion across Christian denominational lines within a small community was an endeavor that once took me a difficult year to organize. Yet Catherine and Gregory knew that this is where deep healing and authentic faith begin – within their own house, and beginning with themselves.

COMPONENTS OF SPIRITUAL MATURITY

Catherine and Gregory were able to discern and to manifest their authentic self in life, in large part due to their spiritual maturity. Although the appearance of mature spirituality will bear a unique face and form depending on the individual, spiritual maturity will entail certain recurring traits and common components. These components, which we will explore further in detail, include:

• *an adult image of God;*

• *knowledge of self;*

• *and the honoring and living out of conscience.*

These components were all part of Catherine's and Gregory's spiritual make-up and life, and were deeply at work in Catherine's literary masterpiece, *The Dialogue*.

The Dialogue is a book that Catherine wrote to address the breadth of her spiritual concerns, which she accomplishes through a series of discourses between the Eternal Father and the human soul (represented by Catherine). In the prologue, Catherine makes four petitions to God: (1) for herself; (2) for the renewal of the Church; (3) for the whole world; and (4) for the assurance of God's wisdom in relationships. The remainder of the book reports God's loving responses to these petitions.

Spiritual maturity crests in full mutuality in relationships, which we will explore with Francis de Sales and Jane de Chantal in the next chapter.

AN ADULT IMAGE OF GOD

What does it mean to say that Catherine and Gregory were operating with an adult, or mature, image of God?

One of the most influential people I encountered during my education at Fordham University was John J. Shea, a professor of pastoral care and counseling. In his work, he asked a key question: If we change as we grow, why does our image of God remain the same? Or does it change and grow too? The question was as simple and direct as a child's, yet it held tremendous implications for individuals as well as corporate bodies of faith and how they interact with each other, both within and beyond their community.

What happens when our image of God remains static through life?

What does it mean for a church to have a static image of God?

In scripture, Jesus refers to himself in so many thought-provoking ways and symbols: he is the Bread of Life, the Gate, the Door, the Vine, the Way, the Shepherd, the Light of the World, the Alpha and Omega, to name but a few. But do our imaginations stay this course? In his book, *Finding God Again*, Shea identifies the unchanging image of God that people and institutions may operate with. He associates it with an adolescing self that aspires toward adulthood but is somehow hindered. This hindrance is what stands in the way of spiritual growth, maturity, imagination, joy, and freedom, the kind of freedom that Catherine and Gregory exercised.

Shea's categories are straightforward, and you might recognize them instantly like a quick mental trip to high school. The childhood or adolescent image of God is that of a supreme being who is often over and against us, like a punishing or rewarding parental figure. The childhood image of God is a God of dependency and control. According to Shea, this is a God of the Group (recall the importance of concurring peers), and a God of Law seeking refuge in dogma and doctrine. And while this may offer us a feeling of clarity, knowing, and safety, we can see how this image of God can take hold in persons as well as parishes for a lifetime. Unless our image of God evolves, we can easily slip into a faith that languishes in church politics or that perceives a congregation as people who are "right" and "wrong." However, as Shea explains, if our imagination of God is free to grow and evolve, an adult self

. . . is able to realize a Living God. The Living God is experienced immediately and directly by the adult self, and each adult self has his or her unique, self-authored, self-owned way of religious experiencing. At the same time, however, there are some definite characteristics of the Living God that can be accurately described. . . . Five such characteristics are offered here, each one reflecting some aspect of how the adult self in integral imaging finds the Living God:

1. *The Living God is a God as Thou.*
2. *The Living God is a God of Love.*
3. *The Living God is a God of Mystery.*
4. *The Living God is a God of Freedom.*
5. *The Living God is a God of Community.*

—JOHN J. SHEA, *Finding God Again*

These are subtle shifts in our understanding and vision that produce enormous changes in our spirituality and approach to life. The adult image of God is one who would not be boxed in, nor would we desire it. Rather, this is a God who would invite us time and again to fall in love with the mystery and beauty of life and creation, whose knowledge is just beyond our reach and who, as Catherine says, "loves us like crazy."

The adult image of God continues to grow and change as we change, and thus remains strongly tied to our imagination, much the way we perceived God as small children.

Very small children have an unfettered image of God that is magical, spontaneous, and changing all the time. God is the sea, the house, Mommy, Daddy, inside, outside; God is us, God is outside of us, God is all around. When my daughter was two years old, she would find a feather at the park by the harbor, a duck or seagull feather, hold it up, and cry out, "Mommy! God is here!" She saw God in feathers for years. When she was six I asked her what God looked like to her, and trying to guess the "right" answer, she replied a little shyly, "An old man?" And I smiled, with the bittersweet advent of growth. The feather, if not gone, had receded.

This is what John Shea refers to when he discusses the "super-ego god" of childhood: god as "an old man"; the god of seeking the right answer; the god of concurring with the group.

But when Jesus says "you must become like a little child" to enter into the kingdom of God, he is pointing to the *little* child, the toddler and her wonderful, imaginative, humorous interpretation of life and people and language, all spouting from the well-spring of love, joy, and wonder . . . with no wrong answers.

What Shea hopes for us in adult spirituality is the return of the feather, if you will, or the rebirth of the liberated mind and unfettered imagination about God, our source and closest friend, but also a great and lovely mystery. Through grace God once again becomes "Thou," or Holy Other.

This is the God of Catherine and Gregory: they are inspired by a God as Thou; they heal through ministries and actions motivated by love; they live in acknowledgment that they will never have all the answers; they seek wisdom from Spirit, and share knowledge with other people in whom they see the Spirit at work; and their goals manifest in community.

KNOWLEDGE OF SELF

Here is the way, if you would come to perfect knowledge and enjoyment of me, eternal Life: Never leave the knowledge of yourself. Then . . . from this knowledge you will draw all that you need. . . . You will find humility in the knowledge of yourself when you see that even your own existence comes not from yourself but from me, for I loved you before you came into being.

—Voice of God, CATHERINE OF SIENNA, *The Dialogue*, 4

Another component of spiritual maturity is knowledge of self, which is entirely in sync with contemporary emphasis on self-awareness, and which is Catherine's cornerstone of continued spiritual development. Nothing proceeds without our continued knowledge of self. Further, the self that Catherine works with, the human being, is not merely good but a wondrous being:

Open your mind's eye and look within me, and you will see
the dignity and beauty of my reasoning creature.

—Voice of God, CATHERINE OF SIENNA, *The Dialogue*, Prologue, 1

This is Catherine's beginning place of self-knowledge, of who we are: an origin defined by dignity and beauty, one not of original sin, but of original grace.

Her quest for self-awareness goes beyond psychology and the emotional life. The self does not exist alone. Catherine gently and artfully explains that in order to truly know who we are, we must look to the one who created us. We are always in relationship. In today's increasingly fragmented world, this may be difficult to remember. But it is imperative to recall and practice. For Catherine, God is at the beginning, the core, and the end of our self-knowledge.

Working with the adult image of the God of Mystery, Catherine acknowledges that while we can make great strides in self-knowledge and awareness, we can never come to a complete understanding of ourselves until we gaze into the "gentle mirror" that is God; that is, until we see ourselves through God's eyes.

What do we see in the mirror, then, we who are made in the divine image?

WAKE-UP CALL: THE DOG OF CONSCIENCE

What fruit do they receive? Pressed by my servants' prayers, I look on them and give them light. I rouse the dog of conscience within them . . . . Sometimes I allow the world to show them its true colors, letting them feel all sorts of emotions, so that they may know how inconstant it is and be more eager to seek their homeland in eternal life.

—God, The Dialogue, 4

Another component of the adult self is the ability to act upon our conscience. We see this in Gregory's decision to return to Rome, come what may. We also see this in Catherine's penchant and ability to speak her mind, or "tell it like it is," through her letters.

In her famous correspondence, Catherine is bold and direct, even rude, often shocking her reader like a chilling wake-up call. She speaks to her addressees bluntly – cardinals, popes, and queens alike – and with great authority. To a cardinal: "You are flowers who shed no perfume, but stench that makes the whole world reek" (Catherine of Siena, *Letters of St. Catherine of Siena*, ed. Vida D. Scudder, p. 278). And to a queen: "You know that you do ill, but like a sick and passionate woman, you let yourself be guided by your passions" (Scudder, p. 287). Her strong words are not always polite, but Catherine is not concerned with being liked. She is beyond that as a spiritual adult. Her desire is to get the job done – to inspire compassion, reconciliation, and peace, no matter the cost.

One of the most important letters Catherine wrote was to Gregory on the subject of peace in Italy. In the letter, she also addressed the issues of corruption in the church and dealing with hypocritical Christians. She appeals to him, as a good shepherd, to imitate Christ, the "First Truth" he is representing. Calling on him to be courageous, she speaks to him as a sideline coach, a worthy opponent, and as a loving daughter, referring to him as "babbo," which means daddy. She calls him on the carpet as the authority over corrupt subordinates, demanding swift and moral corrective action. Catherine writes:

I long to see you the sort of true gentle shepherd who takes an example from the shepherd Christ, whose place you hold . . . . Just so I am begging you, I am telling you, my dear babbo, in the name of Christ crucified, to conquer with kindness, with patience, with humility, with gentleness the wrongdoing and pride of your children who have rebelled against you their father.

I beg you to consider not their wrongdoing but your own kindness.

Take a lesson from the true father and shepherd. For you see that now is the time to give your life for the little sheep who have left the flock.

. . . Help eliminate the vice and sin, the pride and filth that are rampant among the Christian people – especially among the prelates, pastors, and administrators of holy Church who have turned to eating and devouring souls, not converting them but devouring them! And it all comes from their selfish love for themselves, from which pride is born, and greed and avarice and spiritual and bodily impurity.

They see the infernal wolves carrying off their charges and it seems they don't care. Their care has been absorbed in piling up worldly pleasures and enjoyment, approval and praise. And all this comes from their selfish love for themselves. For if they loved themselves for God instead of selfishly, they would be concerned only about God's honor and not their own, for their neighbors' good and not their own self-indulgence. Ah, my dear babbo, see that you attend to these things!

Look for good virtuous men, and put them in charge of the little sheep. Such men will feed in the mystic body of holy Church not as wolves but as lambs. It will be for our good and for your peace and consolation, and they will help you to carry the great burdens I know are yours. It seems to me, gracious father, that you are like a lamb among wolves. But take heart and don't be afraid, for God's prov-

idential help will always be with you. Don't be surprised even though you see a great deal of opposition, and see that human help is failing us, and that those who should be helping us most disappoint us and act against us. Don't be afraid, but even more self-confident; don't give up or restrain your sweet holy desire, but let it be more enkindled with each day that passes.

Up, father!

Up, to give your life for Christ!

Isn't our body the only thing we have?

Peace, peace, peace, my dear babbo, and no more war!

Take courage, take courage, father! Stay away from the bitterness that cripples, but take hold of the bitterness that strengthens . . . in the trust that God will provide for your needs.

—CATHERINE OF SIENA, Letter 74, to
Pope Gregory XI in Avignon

Gregory would respond to the call upon his conscience. Perhaps his colleagues' opinions mattered, but they were not the end factor in his decision-making. He lived in the pope's palace at Avignon, then referred to as "the strongest house in the world." But this house would not be stronger than Gregory's conscience, and it would not take precedence over the greater good that called for unity and renewal and an end to division and war.

He would give up his birthplace, and his family, and further, put an end to his family's historic connection to the papacy. Gregory restored the seat of the church to Rome, and while he would not live to see the conclusion of all the struggles among the Italian states, he spearheaded and put in place the mission of peace that his successor would complete.

BRICKS AND MORTAR: A THEOLOGY OF NEIGHBORS

*. . . It is your duty to love your neighbors as your own self. In love you
ought to help them spiritually and materially in their need – at least
with your good will if you have nothing else. If you do not love me, you
do not love your neighbors, nor will you help those you do not love. But
it is yourself you harm most, because you deprive yourself of grace.*

—God, *The Dialogue*, 6

Catherine and Gregory share a theology of neighbors, born of
their background and upbringing in large families, in large church
communities, in large cities. A sense of solitude and solitary peace
was sought by them through prayer, but their spiritual life and
goals would not end there. They simply never lived or acted
alone. Though strong individuals themselves, and independent
thinkers, their goals were achieved for the sake of community.
Catherine and Gregory always experienced and understood the
interdependence of people, of families, of neighborhoods, of
courts, of city-states, of countries . . . of our world with God. As
a result, their ultimate goal was a community of heaven.

This was displayed through Catherine's work to address
poverty and injustice among the poor of her city, poverty and
injustice that caused her to confront the powers that be.
Although it would not be realized, it was also in her vibrant
imagination to create a papal council, something like King
Arthur's Round Table, except composed of spiritual authorities
rather than knights.

The community of heaven would be apparent in Gregory's
return to Rome, as he chose his eternal home over his earthly

home, his spiritual family above his blood family. The God of community redefines family and reconfigures our relationships and our neighborhoods.

GOD IS THE BRIDGE

As you come to him, the living Stone – rejected by men but chosen by God and precious to him – you, also, like living stones, are being built into a spiritual house . . .

—1 Peter 2:4-5

For years, I have watched my little daughters "climb" up their daddy, my husband; he stands strong, holds their hands high, and their little feet walk up his legs and belly until he pulls them up into an embrace all the way up by his face. He is a living bridge, a steadfast wall that they can scale in complete safety. They trust his strength, and they respond with playful joy.

Like Teresa of Avila, Catherine of Siena utilizes common symbols from daily life to convey her spiritual experiences and ideas in writing. To her, a soul is as a new tree planted in fertile soil. A life of faith is "seasoned," as spice provides both flavor and preservation. And for our connection to the divine love and all its gifts, Catherine utilizes the symbol of the bridge. In *The Dialogue*, God is indeed a bridge over troubled water (Isa. 30:19-21, 43:1-2).

This bridge has walls of stone so that travelers will not be hindered when it rains.

Do you know what stones these are? These are the stones of true solid virtue.

—CATHERINE OF SIENA, *The Dialogue*, 27

In Catherine's time, an important bridge was not thin or delicate as a footbridge. Architecturally, what inspired her vision was most likely expansive, stalwart, a rugged stone bridge with stone walls. In addition to passage, such a bridge also served as a place of gathering, and perhaps even a marketplace with lively merchants and traders along the sides – and so the bridge was a place of community, inviting both those in residence and those passing through.

Catherine is concerned for our spiritual passage, as with any traveler. In *The Dialogue*, God has built a bridge with endearing concern for our safety in bad weather. This is a bridge that protects. And virtue is not an ethereal matter; it is "solid," the muscle, the bricks of spirituality. Virtue is a hard-wearing stepping stone, and the bridge is Christ. He spans not only heaven and earth, but also the distances between people. As she describes, this is a high-arching bridge but also one firmly attached to earth, reflecting the covenant between God and humanity. God is the connection, the beat that pounds out from heart to heart, the breath that inspires soul to soul, and the spark that jumps, illuminating minds.

Importantly, Catherine warns us of the water beneath the bridge:

Those who do not keep to this way travel below to the river – a way not of stones but of water. And since there is no restraining the water, no one can cross through it without drowning.

—The Dialogue, 28

There are many kinds of water in scripture. There are living waters, still waters, waters that cover the sea, daysprings, water that is obedient to Christ, and more. What Catherine creates here is a wonderful metaphor for the waters of life – of how we can get in over our heads, or caught up and swept away by the current which is powerful and unrestrained. We may try to cross these waters of life another way, on our own, beneath the bridge, just as the world offers us many ways of uncertain passage. This is, of course, our choice. What Catherine advises instead, for our sake, is to accept the invitation and the purpose of the bridge, so that we can cross over the sure path that will span all our burdens. She invites us to climb up on our daddy, who is strong enough to carry us, and whose constant safety allows us to journey with paramount joy.

DON'T BURN YOUR BRIDGES

The image of God as a bridge may have influenced Catherine's relationship and interactions with the Florentines as well. When the feud between the city-state and the papacy worsened in 1376, the Signoria, or lordship, of Florence asked Catherine to help influence the pope. She was asked to persuade him to end their excommunication. Because they promised to acquiesce to whatever would be asked of them, toward the aim of reconciliation, Catherine agreed to go to the pope and plead their case.

Unfortunately Catherine was betrayed. She managed to pave the way for the Florentines, in large part due to their pledge of obedience, but at that critical moment, when she had managed to open a door, the Florentines dismissed her and sent in their own ambassadors to negotiate their own terms.

Again, late in 1377, Catherine returned to Florence, once more taking up the cause of creating a lasting peace between that city and Rome. And once again she was used, her good intentions taken advantage of.

Nonetheless, Catherine continued to work and plead for unity and peace. The betrayals angered her, indeed, but she continued to work with the Florentines. Catherine did not burn her bridges, because she knew that the Florentines could not hurt anything in her that mattered. She was not seeking to be liked, appreciated, or even thanked for her intercession. Catherine put her pride aside, laying herself down (herself a bridge between heaven and earth) so that God's peace could be manifested.

AN ETERNAL FLAME

Gregory was an agent of peace but would not live to see it. He succeeded in returning the papacy to Rome but died on March 28, 1378. His task would be completed by his successor, Urban VI.

Catherine died two years later at the tender age of thirty-three on April 29, 1380. She was made a doctor of the church in 1970 (along with Teresa of Avila) and is, among other things, a patroness of Allentown, Pennsylvania – the city that hid the treasure of the Liberty Bell during the Revolutionary War, and that is known for the resolve and spirit of its people during times of change and conflict.

It can be intimidating, even to those privileged with power, to step up to the challenge of conscience. Yet, Gregory and Catherine raised their voices and put actions into being that would help put to right decades of pain and injustice. And it did not matter that they came from opposite ends of the social spectrum – she, just one uneducated girl in a bustling Metropolis, and he, a religious prince born to wealth and power. What mattered was at their center: the light of wisdom, the passion of love, and the eternal flame of hope.

In your nature
eternal Godhead,
I shall come to know my nature.
And what is my nature, boundless love?
It is fire,
because you are nothing but a fire of love.
And you have given humankind
a share in this nature
for by the fire of love
you created us.

—CATHERINE OF SIENA

Love Notes

What We Can Learn from Catherine and Gregory

Mature Image of God

Catherine and Gregory help us to consider our image of God. Our image of God is something that often remains unexplored after a certain age. Rather than encouraging growth and change, we tend to solidify our idea of God into a known entity, an image that we draw on, lean on, and reinforce with time. In some ways, this can be of tremendous value and comfort. But perhaps we shortchange ourselves when we forget all that God is and can be beyond our imagination. How can an evolving image of God help to inform and excite us as we proceed through life's stages?

One of the things I take great pleasure in is teaching and exploring spirituality through forms of popular media. So to further illustrate the development of the adult image of God, let's take a short journey into a fictional future to better understand our present.

To help bring these images into focus, the adolescent and adult images of God and relationship are clear and distinct in two television series: the legendary *Star Trek* series of the 1960s, and its sequel series, *Star Trek: The Next Generation* in the 1980s and

1990s. In many ways, we watch the series and their creators grow up – spiritually, emotionally, and psychologically.

In the first series, Captain Kirk is the law, and stories often revolve around what is right and what is wrong in how others are living. Driven by a more adolescent image of God, the *Enterprise* would venture into the universe seeking out new life-forms, usually to help, change, or conquer them. Kirk tends to act unilaterally, and the series is peppered with his humorous "hirings" and "firings" of the ship's engineer based on his performance in a pinch.

In *The Next Generation*, Captain Picard is no doubt the ship's leader, but relationships are much more lateral than hierarchical. These officers interact as adults in community.

The mature captain is not so solitary a commander. On the bridge, he is bolstered by an empathic counselor at his left hand (Troi) and a first mate at his right (Riker) who resembles Kirk, but whose maturity keeps his passions in check. In this manner, and with this balance, the captain leads impeccably.

The "Prime Directive," virtually the only rule in this mythology, is referred to as a reminder to the crew not to consciously affect change in the societies they encounter or to interfere with their culture.

In the first *Star Trek*, we venture into space to encounter alien beings, or *them*; in *The Next Generation*, we venture into outer space mostly to explore our inner space, us – who we are, and how to best respond and evolve for the greater good. We ask quality-of-life questions: what does it mean to be human, android, imprisoned? What is the role of money in the future, of technology, of sound, of music, of the senses?

This is a giving-way of the God of law and order, to the Living God, God as Thou, the divine cosmic mystery.

The Next Generation's most-repeated phrase – "Engage" – is more than an order; it is an instruction and attitude on how one interacts maturely with the force field of life. We do not seek to rule. We share a dream of community.

Together with the program's other famous phrase, "Make it so," we are then reminded that we are already empowered to fulfill the task.

Integration

In her letter to Gregory, Catherine asks simply, "Isn't our body the only thing we have?" One of our initial passions (and, often, challenges) is our relationship with our body, our physical self. Our parents' attitude toward the body, our own experience of adolescence and emerging sexuality, the messages we receive from our family, culture, and faith – all these can, and hopefully do, lead to wholeness and positive physical and emotional self-esteem.

They may also create divisions and confrontations between the self and body, between mind and the extraordinary instrument that embraces it in this life. And these can be hard to heal. A man can learn to fragment the life force, polarizing God and sex, an enormous schism. A woman may latch onto the goal of "taming" the flesh through diets, of seeking to minimize her physical self, to the extent of being a size zero, double zero, or even minus two.

Why would a person strive to be a zero? Zero implies a complete absence of physical self. Perhaps this is the doctrine held by today's god of the Group.

The mature self is at home in his or her body, comfortable in their own skin and no longer at odds with the body, because the body now defines the self. There is no longer confrontation but integration.

In the case of spiritual maturity, integration extends further to encompass the physical, mental, emotional, and spiritual.

The balance of contemplation and action in the last twelve years of Catherine's life was not merely a relationship of complementarity. She did not pray simply to "refuel" herself for further activity . . . nor was prayer an oasis of rest from work, a kind of holy self-indulgence. It was precisely what she experienced in contemplation that impelled her into action. And all that she touched or was touched by her activity was present in her prayer. . . .

—SUZANNE NOFFKE, O.P., *Catheine of Siena: The Dialogue*

Catherine's prayer life and worldly life became one and the same, no longer diverse or distinct categories, but a weaving, a flowing inward and outward, of love, and knowledge, and next steps, a constant conversation. Her prayer life informed her actions, and her actions in the world informed her prayer life. It is fitting that she named her most influential work *The Dialogue*, for that is what she herself became – a free and flowing dialogue between herself and God.

So much of life's happiness – including fulfillment in our relationships – is rooted in integration, the integration of our dreams and desires with the living out of our daily lives. Does our work resemble our dreams? Does our health reflect our vision of God and Spirit? Does our personal life help to make real our private vision of love on earth?

Explore the ways in which your external living is "in sync" with your internal dialogue, and any disciplines or creative outlets that may help to "bridge" any distances.

Relationship with Neighbors

In a city, one is almost forced to know and interact with one's neighbors, sometimes fleetingly, and sometimes with long-term depth and affection. As we move away from the city centers (for example, away from public transportation and into the private world of the "car culture"), we may become increasingly cut off from those who are, oddly, closest to us physically. Isolation can become a habit of independence. But is this independence real? Consider your relationships with neighbors, to your left, and to your right – at home, at the office, at school, at church. Do you know their joys and troubles? Do they know yours? Do you know their names? Are you in touch only in an emergency?

Our answers to questions like these may reveal how generous we have been with ourselves.

Epilogue

ALL FOR ONE

(Following are two additional reflections inspired by city life, the first focusing on the individual, the second on the masses. Catherine and Gregory loved and served them both.)

It happens every so often in big cities, and it happened here, on this night. Sitting on the subway, going home after a long day at work, a conductor announces over the PA system that we have a sick passenger on the train. It is rush hour. A groan goes up from the masses because we know what that means.

The massive train grinds to a halt at the next station, 34th Street, where we sit for as long as it takes to obtain help for the man, to discern his chest pains and the condition of his heart, to collect the medical personnel to help him from the train to a gurney for transfer according to proper procedures. This could take a while.

We sit, all of us. The entire west side train line has come to a halt. Thousands of New Yorkers are waiting for trains, or are on trains along the line, that have stopped for the incident. There are countless rolling eyes, and pressured sighs, and sarcastic comments, and all manner of frustration onboard.

Yet, this is the barometer of the city: everything must stop for a life. The day that the city doesn't stop for one life, is the day it has lost its soul. And so sitting there on this night, stuck, powerless, late, complaining, and enduring – the disgruntled commuters form a community and a great sign of solidarity and dignity toward the human person.

AND ONE FOR ALL

We walk in sure strides, confident of our environment and the ground beneath our feet, unaware of the true nature of concrete and shoes and earth. Their sub-atomic dance tells another story, one of impermanence, of tendencies to exist and not to exist, of waves of probability – of chance.

—*Dear Little One: Thoughts to My Child*
in an Uncertain World

While it is ideal to gaze into God's gentle mirror to learn our true identity, sometimes the mirror is a sudden and painful one. Nearly every religion has a command similar to Christ's command to love thy neighbor as thyself, but in certain circumstances the understanding of that love becomes crystal clear, and the ability to engage it becomes immediate.

On September 11, 2001, New Yorkers woke up to a usual Tuesday morning, dropping the kids off at school, grabbing coffee on the way to work, writing a last-minute memo on the train into town, stocking shelves, counting money, opening shops and banks and cafés, preparing for a sunny day's work on the verge of autumn. The fall.

Suddenly, the sights and sounds and motions began, like a dream, a bad dream, that had us wondering if we were still asleep as we gaped at an attack on two buildings, two gargantuan towers, straddling downtown like a colossus. And like the great colossus, only the footprints would remain in the soil as the great towers came tumbling down, standing strong as long as possible until they had to breathe their last and collapse like a house of cards upon those neighbors we love.

We watched these events as a world, and those who call the city home watched with the eyes of loving parents. For the city is our child, our beloved and eternal child, one we hope to look at honestly for the good and the bad, to raise well, and to care for.

The tragedy of 9-11 can never be fully expressed, let alone in a few paragraphs in a book. But the enduring power of the day lies in the people, the heart of New York. A theology of neighbors was in full force, as the inhabitants pulled together more than ever. And as strangers tried to save each other, and many lost their lives reaching out the hand of hope to another, they looked into each other's faces and saw very clearly, through the eyes of God, exactly who they were: each other.

They looked in the frightened eyes, and they did not see white or black or Muslim or Christian; they saw parents, babies, and the third graders we all were, together. They saw the human family created by God. And they did not call for war. They did not seek to place blame. They did not confront each other in their diversity from fear and despair. They grieved. This is neighborly love. This is the divine love.

> You will be like a well-watered garden,
>   like a spring whose waters never fail.
> Your people will rebuild the ancient ruins
>   and will raise up the age-old foundations;
>   you will be called Repairer of Broken Walls,
>   Restorer of Streets with Dwellings.
>
> —Isaiah 58:11-12

❖

From this moment my ignorance
closes behind me like the door
through which you entered, recognizing
all I do not know.
And through me you led many people in silence,
many roads, and the turmoil of the streets.

—KAROL WOJTYLA, "Words Spoken by the Woman
at the Well on Departing"

No Holding Back

FRANCIS DE SALES AND JANE DE CHANTAL

Footsteps
St. Malo, France

When I think of my maternal grandfather, Pierre Chappé, I recall a thin, small man who was a giant influence in my early years. In some ways, he was a typical Frenchman; witty, well dressed, with a cigarette dangling straight down from his lips. Somehow he managed to smoke, and to speak, this way. In other ways, he was not so typical. Pépé was a man whose relationships were the stuff of legend.

He was a doctor, the only doctor, in the vicinity of Guignen, Brittany, during World War II. This small village, not far from the university town of Rennes, was occupied by German soldiers, and my grandfather's own stone house was occupied by the S.S. for the duration of the war. He sent my mother, Arlette, then a teenager, away to a Catholic boarding school for her safety. At school, my mother was given a failing grade by a priest for not wearing the proper uniform in gym class. Given the deeply trying and emotional events taking place at the time, Dr. Chappé went to the convent and flattened the priest with a single right hook. My mother said that she would rather be home with the S.S. than remain with the nuns, and so my grandfather brought her home.

At home, the roles and tensions my grandfather endured were enormous. His home was occupied, yet he was a member of the Resistance. He provided medical care to the French soldiers who were wounded. But he would also tend to the wounded Germans. He would travel through fields of mud and manure in the middle of the night to delivery a baby at a farm, receiving as payment a chicken or loaf of bread. And for him that was payment enough. People began to bring their children to my grandfather to be baptized.

His relationship with me began much later, when he was retired to the seaside in St. Malo, a wonderful fortified city on the coast of Brittany. Then, in the 1960s, I was his towhead American granddaughter visiting from New York to spend the summer with him. I spoke very little French at the time, and he very little English. And yet we sat together beside his large picture window in the afternoons, gazing at each other, playing, and enjoying a deeply intuitive, mutual love.

Although we could not speak to each other very much, he could still share with me what he learned about life. And one day, when I was five years old, he taught me something I would not forget – how to cook and eat artichokes, which grow abundantly in Brittany.

First, I watched as he prepared them by snipping the sharp points atop the outer leaves. Then he leveled them underneath with a knife so that they would sit straight in a pot of seasoned boiling water. Next, we put them in the pot, which held four artichokes. Then we cooked them for about forty minutes. Afterwards, they had to cool down, so some patience was required.

Finally, we sat down together at the kitchen table with an artichoke between us. We began by gently pulling off the tougher outer leaves, one by one, enjoying the tiny bit of "meat" they bestowed, and then tossing the leaves in a large bowl. A little deeper into the artichoke the leaves grew finer, and there was more to eat from their base. Deeper still, the leaves became thin, delicate, and so tender that one could consume them almost in entirety. Finally, the smallest remaining leaves swirled tightly together in a point shaped like a tiny wizard's hat and could be pulled away from the heart in one piece.

Then came the challenge. Around the heart was a layer of fine yet prickly fair "hair" that needed to be pulled off between tight fingertips or gently scraped away so as not to damage the heart. It was painstaking for me as a young child, but we persevered and revealed the hidden treasure – the tender heart. The moment arrived: I dipped the meat into a perfect vinaigrette and sank my teeth into the heart's nutlike goodness, golden oil running down my chin. Pépé smiled. He knew all about clearing the way to the heart.

When it comes to work, various life issues, and even the human psyche, the onion is traditionally cited as a symbol or analogy – that is, there are layers and layers to peel away in order to get to the center. But the nature of the onion remains essentially the same throughout.

When it comes to love, I prefer the symbol of the artichoke: there are different stages on the journey to its heart. The artichoke requires persistence and patience. Like love, it holds a gift that calls for a special effort, and we may stop short in our relationships if we find the final layer, or barrier, too difficult or demanding or distasteful. But if we choose to stop – and so many of us do – we will cheat ourselves of the grandest prize.

Francis de Sales and Jane de Chantal were French missionaries who brought a renewed experience of faith to their own compatriots throughout France. They met as a result of grief and loss, and they learned that the way forward through the modern era was the way of the heart – the unobstructed heart, free to love in peace and full mutuality.

No Holding Back

There is no holding back, no careful distance,
no concern about possible misinterpretations,
no fear for too much too soon.

—HENRI J. M. NOUWEN, on the relationship
between Francis and Jane

The story of Francis de Sales and Jane de Chantal is one of opening the floodgates of Spirit, of letting the rivers of human emotion and thought flow freely, until they run their complete course,

(copyright De Sales Spirituality Center)

splashing in the freedom and safety of trust, and sparkling in the joy and comfort of peace. The relationship of these seventeenth-century saints is marked by an exquisite correspondence, one that puts on the table all that needs to be said and felt regarding their spiritual awakening and life, because there was so much to say, and so much to feel!

Christianity is so often a story of newness, of new wine and new wineskins, of second chances, close shaves, of beginning again from a new perspective, and with a renewed heart. Francis de Sales experienced this newness, and so did Jane de Chantal, though in different ways.

Francis was always called to the church, but he would experience a spiritual crisis about God and the new concept of predestination that would become his pivotal challenge as a young man.

Jane, a wife and mother in a happy marriage, would lose her beloved husband in an accident – and from her grief, would begin to seek out new meaning and a new way of life. Francis and Jane were two people in a process of growth; and they would find the road to God in each other, stepping sprightly on each other's inner pathways with sureness of stride.

THE MAN

In 1567, Francis de Sales was born in the family castle, the Chateau of Thorens, in Savoy, an independent duchy that shared borders with France, Italy, and Switzerland and that was eventually annexed by France in 1860. Typically, his parents hoped that their son would pursue a sturdy and profitable career, such as law or politics, in order to carry on the strong family line. As he grew, Francis tried to please his parents as long as he was able, even earning his law doctorate at the University of Padua. When he returned home from studies, he was poised to begin a position as Senate advocate.

But Francis was a person known for his kindness and gentle ways. And those gentle ways would eventually win over his family when he could walk their path no more, when they opposed his surrender and confession to the call to the priesthood.

His gentle ways with others, and his ability to communicate the church doctrine simply and clearly, also brought many people into (and back to) the church.

Now living out his authentic life's work, Francis became bishop of Geneva at the age of thirty-five. He especially enjoyed traveling and preaching in his native Duchy of Savoy. He would become a prolific writer and correspondent. After this life's work, he would become a doctor of the church and the patron saint of all writers and educators. He loved children.

He would meet a woman with four children, and together they would found the Order of the Visitation, from the deepest heart of their loving partnership.

Every moment comes to us pregnant with a command from God,

only to pass on and plunge into eternity,

there to remain forever what we have made of it.

—FRANCIS DE SALES

THE WOMAN

Five years after Francis de Sales came into the world, a baby girl was born on January 28, 1572, to a prominent family at Dijon, France. She was Jeanne Frances Fremyot, the daughter of the president of parliament of Burgundy.

She would not know her mother for very long – sadly she would die when Jane was only eighteen months old – and her father would raise her alone to the best of his ability.

At the age of twenty, Jane married Christopher de Rabutin, Baron de Chantal. They had six children, though only four survived into adulthood. They loved each other and enjoyed a happy marriage.

One day in 1601, when she was only twenty-nine years old, Jane received word that her husband had been shot by a family friend in a tragic hunting accident. He was mortally wounded; Christopher died in her arms.

In some ways, Jane was like the woman at the well in the fourth chapter of the Gospel of John. She was a woman who had married, had lost that bond through circumstances beyond her control, and could not return home again. She was trying to get on as best she could, but in her grief, increasing loneliness, and isolation, she was beginning to question her life and the meaning of faith. What would become of her?

> *When we are at a loss what to do,*
> *when human help fails us in our dilemmas,*
> *then God inspires us . . .*
>
> —FRANCIS DE SALES, *Finding God Wherever You Are*

Jane, a young widow with four children, faced an open future. For some time, the grieving family lived with her father-in-law. During this time, Jane learned that the financial affairs of the estate were in tatters, and she set to work to put the estate back on track. Perhaps this project kept her going through this terribly difficult period of mourning. A fine administrator, Jane was able to manage and nourish the estate back to financial health, thus ensuring the security of her children. Once that was in place, her duty done, it seems her emotions were able to surface once more, and she became desolate.

After three years had passed, Jane met Francis de Sales in Dijon when he was a young bishop preaching during Lent of 1604. Francis was on fire for God and he stressed the importance (and the possibility) of finding God right where we are, at any place, at any time, and under any circumstances. The two were deeply impacted by each other, and she sought his spiritual direction in her grief. Their model relationship is renowned for its honesty, passion, and of course its famous correspondence.

At the same time the New World was being discovered across a vast ocean, Jane and Francis were building their own new world at home, one soul at a time. Then in 1610, Jane founded the Congregation of the Visitation of Holy Mary, also known as the Order of the Visitation, at Annecy. Their order reflected the modern era that was being born. With inclusiveness and mutuality at its heart, the Visitandines welcomed widows, those of delicate health, the aged, and the physically challenged. Jane understood these things: no one need be left behind.

Francis passed away in 1622. More than eighty communities were in place nearly twenty years later when Jane died in the Visitation convent at Moulins. Jane de Chantal was buried at Annecy near the body of her trusted friend Francis. She is the patroness of widows, forgotten people, and those who have lost parents.

> *Simplicity towards God consists in seeking Him only in all our actions,*
> *whether we are going to the office, dining room, or recreation;*
> *let us go everywhere to seek God and to obey God.*
>
> —JANE DE CHANTAL

AN EXTRAORDINARY OPPORTUNITY

What the founding of the Visitandine order offered Jane was an extraordinary opportunity to achieve something here and now, with what she had received from life thus far, and what she had to give – a core component of Salesian spirituality. When emerging from her grief, Jane had come to realize that she would not seek to marry again. Instead, she would seek to immerse herself completely in a life of love, praise, and service to God. With Francis, she was able to accomplish this while still young.

Traditionally, someone in Jane's position would wait for the "empty nest" – when the last of her children had grown to adult-hood – to finally attend and commit to her spiritual life. But through Francis, Jane was able to bring her youngest daughter, Françoise, with her into the community. She would be able to raise her there, while continuing to build the order and live out her calling. This example shows us how the order perceived not only women but also children – not as a mere distraction, but as an important part of our human family. Jane was allowed to be a mother at work. This was a tremendous gift as well as a signpost of the modern world to come.

GOD EMERGES FROM THE TEMPLE

*The glory of Yahweh then came out over the temple threshold and
paused over the cherubim.*

—Ezekiel 10:18

The Visitation of Holy Mary was a community created for women
who felt called to the religious life but who did not necessarily
possess the youth, strength, or complete liberty from family
responsibilities traditionally required to make this kind of life
commitment. Further, these were women who, when faced with
the options of rigorous religious orders and the physical austeri-
ties they espoused, were seeking something else, another way of
life, and a gentler form of religious expression.

Francis and Jane would not encourage people to bring their
vibrant devotion to an austere house; instead, they would turn
this example around – and nurture a spirituality written on the
heart, an embodied ascetic faith rooted in friendship and charity
that would be brought out into the world and lived in every corner of life. With Francis and Jane, God is experienced not only
in church; God comes out of the temple and into the streets, the
office, the shops, the schools. We see this in their correspondence, especially in Jane's letters to family, sisters, bishops, and
other members of society. Her spiritual direction embraces the
gamut of experience, from advice on communion, prayer, and daily
habits, to weddings, money, pregnancy, and bereavement. They
understand that God is at the center of our life and all our relationships.

THE CLEAR MIRROR

As often as you can during the day, recall your mind to the presence of God.... Consider what God is doing, what you are doing. You will always find God's eyes fixed on you in unchangeable love.

—FRANCIS DE SALES

We are beginning to realize, from the texts of so many contemplatives as well as pediatricians and psychologists, the vastly important presence of the mirror during our formative years – not just any mirror – the holy mirror, the reflection that is clear and clean and containing an image of reality.

From behavioral science, we have learned that parents need to mirror an infant's expressions, sounds, and emotions, so that the baby's actions toward growth are acknowledged, reinforced, and encouraged. From books such as Alice Miller's *The Drama of the Gifted Child*, we explore what might occur when the mother does not mirror her child appropriately; the child may develop a personality that seeks Mom's attention and approval, and this personality acts as a kind of mask. It is not the authentic self.

Many monastic traditions have within them a philosophy and spiritual practice of cleaning or polishing a mirror daily. The spotless mirror shows us the self as it is – unfettered, unobstructed, and unadorned. Of course this may frighten many who are uncertain what that sort of mirror would reflect! That is all right too. For growth, a clear image of our person, life, source, and condition, here and now, is necessary.

In psychological circles, we learn of "unconditional positive regard," the nonjudgmental response to information shared in a session or between any two people engaged in an intimate discussion. Unconditional positive regard is the mirror that gives us that feeling of safety that glows between friends, bolsters strong spouses, and strengthens trusted colleagues. It is also at the heart of the adage "Hate the sin, not the sinner." Unconditional positive regard works with the basic fact that people are good at heart, and that most are operating with the best of intentions. We rise. We fall. We rise again, with the help of God and our friends. We are human and imperfect. It is all right. All is well.

This mirror is what Francis de Sales shared with Jane de Chantal. They shared not only their passion for God, but also their yearnings for growth, their obstacles, their fears, their losses, their findings, their work, their spiritual and life-living tools, their love for each other – their entire process. The mutuality they shared with each other embodied the covenant God shares with us. And that is the greatest gift of a fully actualized relationship.

LETTER WRITING

The way this mirror was reflected most often was through their correspondence. In this day and age, when we rarely communicate by handwritten letters, it may seem a cumbersome or romantic endeavor to haul out the fine paper and pens. But Francis wrote over four hundred letters to Jane. Consider how letter writing may be a form of prayer, or spiritual journaling – journaling to another. It is a different way of communicating; its intimacy and personality are not so easily attained or captured today, given the ease and immediacy of electronic media.

For example: I am right-handed for the most part – I throw right-handed, sew right-handed, stir sauce in a pot right-handed, play tennis right-handed – except when I pick up a pen to write something; I write with my left hand. And when I sit down to write something by hand, a shift occurs, and I begin utilizing a different part of my brain, literally accessing a different place, a different way of thinking, a different connection with my world, and different words. Poems especially come from my left hand (or the right side of my brain). I cannot create poetry on a computer keyboard. I can edit it there, but I cannot create it – it is tapped from a different source, one that also has a timelessness and mystery about it, even to me.

This is what the experience of letter writing offered Francis and Jane, and continues to offer us today. When we sit down to write to someone we care for, we enter into another space, one akin to prayer. It is a commitment, and it requires some solitude. All at once we peruse our thoughts:

What is important?

What do I really want or need to share?

What events have transpired that affect my life, and those around me?

What remains unchanging, like our affection?

What makes me laugh?

What would make my friend laugh?

When we write a letter to a trusted friend, we share the account of our life and, either consciously or unconsciously, we show how God is working through it. Add to this some methods of personal improvement, and we begin to see the wealth of unedited information shared by Francis and Jane. When we write a letter, we are also writing to the God of joy and mystery, much the way we did with pen pals as children. There is just something magical about a personal letter from a friend appearing in the mail. And this was the primary form of spiritual direction chosen by Francis and Jane – years of correspondence that would be their way of sharing and learning – forming and honing them both.

What is unique in the correspondence of Francis de Sales and Jane de Chantal is the degree of freedom of expression they enjoy with regard to the affection they feel for each other's person and journey. In this day of correct, even sterile, behavior between colleagues (especially in the church) in an increasingly litigious society, it is wonderful and refreshing to find two people who can express their love and affection for each other with such openness and freedom:

I know you have complete confidence in my affection; I have no doubt about this and delight in the thought. I want you to know and to believe that I have an intense and very special desire to serve you with all my strength. It would be impossible for me to explain either the quality or the greatness of this desire that

I have to be at your spiritual service, but I can tell you that I believe you that it is from God, and for that reason, I cherish it and every day see it growing and increasingly remarkably.

All other bonds are temporal, even that of a vow of obedience which can be broken through death or other circumstances; but the bond of love grows and gets even stronger with time. It cannot be cut down by death, which, like a scythe, mows down everything but charity.

I never say holy mass without you and those closest to you; I never receive communion without you, and finally, I am as much yours as you could ever wish me to be.

—FRANCIS OF ASSISI, Letter to Jane, June 24, 1604

God gave me a tremendous love for your soul. As you became more and more open with me, a marvelous obligation arose for my soul to love yours more and more; that is why I was prompted to write you that God had given me to you. I didn't believe that anything could be added to the affection I felt for you, especially when I was praying for you. But now, my dear daughter, a new quality has been added – I don't know what to call it. All I can say is that its effect is a great inner delight which I feel. I wish you the perfect love of God and other spiritual blessings.

I never pray without including you in my petitions; I never greet my own angels without greeting yours. Do the same for me, and get [your son] to pray for me also. I always pray for him and all your little family. You may be sure that I never forget them in my mass, nor their deceased father, your husband.

—FRANCIS OF ASSISI, Letter to Jane, October 14, 1604

Their letters to each other were only the beginning of their spiritual communication. From this central font of guidance and mutual support came many other spiritual friendships and corre-

spondences of spiritual direction with diverse men and women –
all rooted in this same divine and mutual love and support.

SPIRITUAL DIRECTION

*Guides proclaim good news; they respect the dignity of every human being;
they call us into repentance. Guides break bread and serve the Christ in all
persons, extending God's hand of invitation. They pass on the spark of creation but do not get in the way. Each of us is both guide and guided . . . .*

—CAROLINE WESTERHOFF

Spiritual direction is a mutual process, and primarily one of listening. As discussed previously in the chapter on Francis and Clare
of Assisi, the root of the words "obey" and "obedience" comes
from a word meaning to listen or to give ear. When engaged in
spiritual direction, we listen to another's journey, gathering pic-
tures of how God is leading and being manifested along the path,
getting a sense of obstacles or roadblocks, as well as new paths.
We also share joy, humor, sadness, hope, Spirit, and silence. It is
an intuitive discernment process, full of meaning, and its purpose
is to help uncover and manifest the directee's authentic self, while
identifying aspects of his or her life that may not be helpful. Like
prayer, spiritual direction is an opportunity to listen . . . to invite
. . . to see . . . and to take in the breath of spirit.

Regarding Francis and Jane, there is a pattern in their letters
of spiritual direction – basic spiritual "housekeeping," prayer,
meditations, and suggestions for readings and practices. But there
is also the personal and intimate sharing about love, growth, and
life in God – how the spiritual journey is unique to each of us, and
how we require our own approach. As Francis explains,

The practice of devotion must be adapted to the strength, to the occupation and to the duties of each one in particular.

Moreover, just as every sort of gem, cast in honey, becomes brighter and more sparkling, each according to its color, so each person becomes more acceptable and fitting in his own vocation when he sets his vocation in the context of devotion. Through devotion your family cares become more peaceful, mutual love between husband and wife becomes more sincere . . . and our work, no matter what it is, becomes more pleasant and agreeable.

—FRANCIS DE SALES, Introduction to *The Devout Life*

This desire of yours [to grow spiritually] should be like orange trees along the sea coast of Genoa which almost all year long are covered with fruit, blossoms and leaves all at the same time.

Every day presents occasions for your desire to ripen, so you should bear fruit constantly; yet, you should never stop hoping for further opportunities to advance. Such longings are the blossoms of the tree of your desire.

—FRANCIS OF ASSISI, Letter to Jane, May 3, 1604

Rather than wash away our diversity toward a goal of uniformity of service, Francis would have us discern and implement our particular strengths and interests through spiritual direction. This approach recognizes and nurtures our gifts and abilities, as St. Paul said, bringing out the maximum helpfulness, value, and fulfillment in the body of Christ, or in any fellowship. Nurturing our gifts and abilities enables us to become our authentic selves — and any step toward personal authenticity improves community. Further, each day brings opportunity for reflection, growth, and loving action. However, we must make room for it through awareness.

SOLITUDE

It is good when a soul loves solitude; it's a sign that it takes delight in God and enjoys speaking with him.

—JANE DE CHANTAL

Remember frequently to retire into the solitude of your heart, even while you are externally occupied in business or society. This mental solitude need not be hindered even though many people may be around you, for they surround your body not your heart, which should remain alone in the presence of God.

—FRANCIS DE SALES.

Although we do not need to be alone in order to experience some heavenly solitude, it helps. And when we finally do get some quality "alone time," as my children call it, it is imperative to unplug.

These days, it is rare to see people truly enjoying solitude. Every day, and in every place, we see people going about their solitary tasks on the phone. Driving. Shopping. Walking in town. Everywhere we go, there seems to be a cell phone or headset permanently attached to someone's hand or ear. St. Augustine suggested that the hands need to be empty to experience our surroundings, and to be free to better receive God's graces. Today, I would add that the ear that is filled with noise cannot hear. Simply, when constantly on a cell phone, a person is not present.

When on the phone, the young mother is not present to her child and her child's point of view, as she pushes the stroller. She does not see what he or she is noticing in the world. While on the phone, the person walking for exercise is not aware of his breath or the sound of his cross trainers on the sidewalk. While on the phone, the retiree at the harbor is not present to enjoy fully the stunning view of islands, lighthouses, and majestic clouds before him. He is not aware of the people around him, or the child trying to show him a seashell. He is not there. We are fast becoming a culture that is constantly chatting about something and rarely listening.

To distill the value from any activity, we must be present to it. We must give our whole self to our alone time, regardless of the task. We are worth it. We can receive wonderful insights through silence when we garden, when we do the laundry, or when we take a walk. But we need to be silent. We need to get off the phone.

When we are silent, truly in the nurturing gift of our solitude, we are able to connect with our environment. We are able to notice things that are more symbolic – a bird, a kind of flower, the wind, shadows – and we are able to "hear" our inner voice and the larger voice of nature. The Spirit speaks in many ways and through many things all around us. We give generously to ourselves when we allow the enclosure of solitude to inform, refuel, and nourish us. It also connects us more easily to the things that are eternal.

FINALLY – MUTUALITY

Mutuality is the word here . . . A mutual openness, a mutual sharing, a mutual confession of needs, a mutual confession of forgiveness, a mutual knowing of being known – that is the source of community where God's strength is made manifest . . .

—HENRI J. M. NOUWEN

By giving yourself to God, you not only receive Himself in exchange, but eternal life as well.

—FRANCIS DE SALES

Mutuality is the source and the gift, the ultimate expression of love in relationship. It is at the heart of creation, of life coming into being and giving back, again and again. It is in the balance of all creatures living together within every kind of ecosystem. Similarly, when we are in relationship, all of life is best served by the act of mutuality. Mutuality is an action – not merely a philosophy – and it is a way of living that in many ways determines our quality of life.

We can all become involved with a lover; we can all get married; we can all partner up in business; and we can all have a friend. But the depth and degree of satisfaction gained from these bonds will depend largely on whether both people are engaged in the relationship with mutual interest, honesty, and communication. That is how we honor each other. And very often, as the saying goes, "God is in the details."

Some plants point their flowers at the sun, and turn them with it as it moves. The sunflower, however, turns not only its flowers, but its leaves as well.

—FRANCIS DE SALES, *Finding God Wherever You Are*

The experience of mutuality, or the lack of it, can be difficult for many to discern. Its presence or absence can be subtle in our day-to-day living. But mutuality is a quality that makes our love vibrant, taking it from ordinary to extraordinary. It is at the core of intimacy, and it stems from primacy of the relationship.

True love demands primacy. Once, I attended a weekend seminar of Engaged Encounter, a retreat for engaged couples that grew out of the Marriage Encounter movement. At one session, a priest asked the roomful of couples, "Do you have any friends who want to see you by yourself, without your fiancé, who do not seem to encourage your relationship?" Many looks went around the room, hands were raised, and some people smiled or chuckled about this scenario in their lives. The priest replied curtly, "You better get new friends." The room fell silent with his gravity and the gravity of the issue which the couples perhaps did not realize. Or perhaps they realized it was somehow a thorn in their side, but did not know why. This is why: if we are getting married, we must put our marriage first. A shift of axis must take place in our relationships in order to achieve fullness of mutuality and intimacy.

Full mutuality and intimacy may take root and flourish through this shift of axis – one that aligns the relationship as the central point around which all other events and concerns revolve. Further, it helps if this shift is the center of how we percieve our time. I once drew something on a paper napkin in a café that my husband still carries around with him nearly a decade later. The drawing illustrates two ways of considering our daily schedule.

We, especially in the West, may perceive our day in linear terms:‹

Commute ➤ Work ➤ School ➤ Gym Class ➤ Commute ➤ Home/Relationship

That is, our relationship is the goal we get to at the end of the day, only after we have taken care of everything else, finished our work, and completed our tasks. Then we can get to our loved one. But there is another way of considering time and looking at our day, and it looks a little more like a wheel:

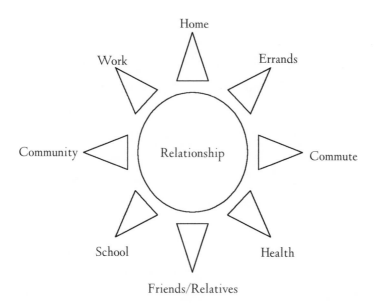

When we keep our love relationship at the center of our daily consciousness, then it is no longer lived out at the end of the day or in our free time. It is something we continuously carry with us. Further, when our relationship is the center around which all external events revolve, we become stronger, we continue to bear witness to our love, and we feel connected and protected. We share all things. Our relationship becomes the lens through which we see our world and the anchor that holds us steady in the face of the events of life. Our partner accompanies us through all our work, cares, and tasks, even when we are not sharing the same physical space; in this way, our personal relationship imitates our bond with God. Jesus said, "I am with you always."

From this place, from the centering of our love, mutuality occurs through intimacy – the knowing of each other's stories, each other's tastes, each other's fears and dreams, favorite pleasures, important beliefs, and formative experiences, both good and bad. Intimacy is also in the smaller things, such as partners knowing how each spends the day. This kind of knowing occurs through listening. When we truly listen to holy other, we take him or her in, as we take in a child from the rain, all wrapped up in loving arms. When we truly hear someone, we want to help and to fulfill needs.

As the sunflower turns its whole being toward the light of the sun, not only its face, this is how we must turn our selves to each other as partners – entirely – not merely to honor the most basic vows between us, but with our hearts and our will turned to face the light of our relationship. In this light, we will grow. We will grow toward and with God, together.

A SPIRITUALITY FOR ALL TIMES

Let us belong to God . . . in the midst of so much busyness,
brought on by the diversity of worldly things.

—FRANCIS OF ASSISI

Let us be what we are, and be that well, in order to bring honor
to the Master Craftsman whose handiwork we are.

—FRANCIS OF ASSISI

Francis de Sales and Jane de Chantal lived on the threshold of modernity. The world at large had seen tremendous paradigm shifts that literally rocked their consciousness. Science had revealed that the earth revolved around the sun, not the sun around the earth. The Renaissance had created the world's most astounding endeavors in the arts. Now the discovery of the New World proved not only that other lands and peoples existed, but that we would not fall off the edge of the earth if we sailed too far. The old myths and superstitions were beginning to pass away, and a new day was dawning, one of new human awareness. And their spirituality reflects their adaptability to this new world.

Emerging from this arena of change, the Salesian spirit is one that embraces our imperfections in an uncertain world. Francis and Jane welcome us, come-as-you-are, to the great and timeless invitation of God. And they extend that invitation to everyone. In this time and place, it is not only the religious who are called. Francis and Jane would say we are all called.

Importantly, Salesian spirituality embraces a gentle approach to faith and spiritual growth, one that encourages care and patience as perhaps the greatest tools on the journey. As Francis explains, and Jane concurs,

Yes, truly, ever so gently we must continue to cut out of our lives all that is superfluous . . . Don't you see that no one prunes vines by hacking them with an axe but by cutting them very carefully with a pruning hook, one shoot at a time?

—FRANCIS OF ASSISI, Letter to Mme. de Limojon, June 28, 1605

However, should you fall even fifty times a day, never, on any account, should that surprise or worry you. Instead, ever so gently set your heart in the right direction and practice the opposite virtue. . . . No matter what happens, be gentle and patient with yourself.

—JANE DE CHANTAL, Letter to Sr. Peronne-Marie de Châtel, February 9, 1616

Remarkably, when we examine the expanse of their writings, we see that Francis's and Jane's insights extend centuries ahead of them. They intuit aspects of our lives and challenges today that are astounding – keen insights into psychology and social challenges that are completely in tune with present-day ailments, concerns, and even Twelve Step programs of recovery and healing.

Francis on anxiety and depression:

There is a real temptation to become dissatisfied with the world and depressed about it when we have of necessity to be in it. God's providence is wiser than we.

—FRANCIS, Letter to Mme. de la Fléchère, January 20, 1609

Anxiety is a temptation in itself and also the source from and by which other temptations come.

Sadness is that mental pain which is caused by the involuntary evils which affect us. These may be external—such as poverty, sickness—or they may be internal—such as ignorance, dryness in prayer, aversion, and temptation itself.

When the soul is conscious of some evil, it is dissatisfied . . . and sadness is produced. The soul wishes to be free from this sadness, and tries to find the means for this.

If the soul seeks deliverance for the love of God, it will seek with patience, gentleness, humility, and calmness, waiting on God's providence rather than relying on its own initiative. . . .

Anxiety comes from an irregulated desire to be delivered from the evil we experience. Therefore, above all else, calm and compose your mind. Gently and quietly pursue your aim.

—FRANCIS OF ASSISI, *Daily Readings with St. Francis de Sales*

Jane on forgiveness:

If we wish to remove all barriers to grace in preparation for receiving the great fruits of prayer, we must forgive everyone unreservedly.

—Exhortation 13, March 23, 1630, on the 20th Chapter of the Rule

Jane on amends:

Gentle love scatters abroad an aura of joy and peace. That is why we try to cherish and please our neighbor. To remain openhearted we must forgive ourselves when we fall and courageously make amends with loving patience. By persevering in such actions, we eventually will be given humble, gracious, and pliable hearts which will enable us to render great services to our Lord.

—Conference 22: "On the advantages and the dangers of a compliant nature, and on the happiness of being employed in lowly offices"

Jane on placing "principles above personalities":

Cordial love of the neighbor does not consist in feelings. This love flows not from a heart of flesh but from the heart of our will. We must stop twisting and turning about to discover what we like or dislike. Whether we experience aversion or inclination for something really does not matter, provided only that in our wills, we remain firm and unswerving in pure love. Then we will give God proofs of love amidst the strongest distastes and aversions as well as during consolations and sensible love. Only if we proceed in this way will we improve!

—Conference 10: "On the true Supernatural life and meekly bearing with our neighbor"

Francis on "God's will, not ours":

Our greatest fault is that we wish to serve God in our way, not in His way – according to our will, not according to His will. When He wishes us to be sick, we wish to be well; when He desires us to serve Him by sufferings, we desire to serve Him by works; when He wishes us to exercise charity, we wish to exercise humility; when He seeks from us resignation, we wish for devotion, a spirit of prayer or some other virtue. And this is not because the things we desire may be more pleasing to Him, but because they are more to our taste. This is certainly the greatest obstacle we can raise to our own perfection. . . .

Francis on working the steps of new life:

God not only means us to be saved, but actually gives us all we need to achieve salvation. So we are not to stop at merely desiring salvation, but go a step further . . .

It is all very well to say, "I want to be saved." It is not much use merely saying, "I want to take the necessary steps." We must actually take the steps. We need to make a definite resolution . . . and use the graces God holds out to us. . . . That is why general acts of devotion and prayer should always be followed by particular resolutions.

—FRANCIS OF ASSISI, *Treatise on the Love of God*, Book 8, Chap. 4

Francis and Jane also show us that, although we tend to consider our trials as uniquely modern, due to our increasingly changing, technological, and uncertain world, anxiety, depression, and other issues have been around for quite some time; they are not new to the human condition. And so Francis and Jane tap into a greater awareness of what it is to be human, and in their blessed mutuality, continue the dialogue with us now – four hundred years later.

BEGIN WITH TODAY

Look straight in front of you and not at those dangers you see in the distance. . . . They look like armies, but they are only willow branches. Let us think of living only today well, and when tomorrow comes, it will also be today and we can think about it then.

—FRANCIS OF ASSISI, Letter to Mlle. De Soulfour,

July 22, 1603

It is at the core of Salesian spirituality to begin with today, and with the facts of our life at hand, such as they are, to seek God. We look for God in this moment, with what we have, no more, no less. We are acceptable as we are today. There is no need to acquire or improve traits, or to lose any. And we can find God in everything. God is here. Hope is here. Love is here, in everything we do, in every corner of our daily life. And so we return to the beginning:

Your life is holy, and your love is holy. Your breakfast rush, your kids on their way to school, your daily commute, your eyes made tired by the PC, your wondering about what dinner to make, your wondering about which bills to pay, your perpetual pile of waiting laundry – all holy.

GOD'S GOOD TIME

Finally, I would like to close with a letter that Jane de Chantal wrote to a prospective member of her community, four centuries ago.

Jane often did not date her letters. Perhaps that is no coincidence; her love and words are timeless, as are the joy and invitation of Spirit. And so I dedicate this letter to you.

Dear Reader,

Although I have never met you, I know you and love you very much.

Do everything you are taught in a spirit of gentleness and fidelity in order to reach the goal toward which you are being guided, cutting short all thought of attaining it except in God's good time. . . . Then set to work . . . and lovingly resolve to serve God in this way, desiring nothing more.

If you do this, you will soon find yourself in that state of tranquility and peace which is so necessary for souls who wish to live virtuously, according to the spirit, and not according to their own inclinations and judgments.

This is what I see to be necessary for your peace of mind and spiritual advancement. May God fill each one of us with Himself. . . . I am yours with love.

Jane de Chantal

Love Notes

What We Can Learn from Francis and Jane

Communication

In a world in which communication has become immediate, electronic, momentary, and fleeting, it may be difficult to recall that all we really have is what we communicate to each other. In the end, what we have said (or not said) is what we leave behind; what we share with our children, what we confide in our spouse, what we impart to community, can be our greatest legacy or a thorn of despair, depending on whether we answer the call to communicate.

Francis and Jane demonstrate through the power of their letters that an intimate correspondence can more than survive the test of time. It is their documentation of and ode to human spiritual love and growth. We get to know each other through our communication, and we get to hone each other. Francis and Jane made their communication a form of prayer. This may continue in our own lives as well. Spouses may continue to write love letters to each other, parents can write to their children, and so on.

Keep a Prayer Journal

One of the best ways to enter a meditative practice is to keep a prayer journal. Anyone can learn to relish this delicious approach to prayer – and everyone can reap its soulful benefits. Some of the best snapshots in my mind's eye have been taken while writing in my prayer journal. I have written in the hazy morning, and at starry night; inside by a crackling fire; outside in the cold, watching Comet Hale-Bopp by candlelight. I have placed flowers in my journal, and autumn leaves, and a lock of my toddler's hair. Of course the most important aspect is the content of the journal, the prayers themselves, the thoughts and reflections of your life, your joys and sorrows, your world – all immersed within your relationship with God.

More, you will be able to see how you have grown spiritually when reviewing older journals – how the things you pray about, and how you pray, have evolved over time.

If you haven't kept a journal before, you may want to buy a special journaling book at a local stationery or book store. This is a tactile activity, so the book should be of a texture, color, or pattern that resonates with you. This will be your special book, your keeper of sacred communication.

Like any form of prayer, your new practice will grow deeper if you set aside a time and place each day that is just for this, just for you. A quiet place works well, but you do not have to be alone. The morning commute, if you find yourself sitting on a train or bus for more than fifteen minutes, provides a wonderful opportunity to get centered and greet the day with some spiritual observation and connection. Conversely, the commute home offers the opportunity to "debrief" your spirit and the events and challenges of the day.

I usually begin writing from a place of gratitude, noting the weather, landscape, or other surroundings. The real joy is simply writing from your heart. Trust yourself. Honor your feelings. Be gentle with yourself. And listen.

Mutuality

Full mutuality is at the core of romantic love and spiritual love, and it can be a barometer that attests to the fullness of a relationship. Mutuality refers to reciprocal openness in communication, mutual validation, mutual support, mutual respect, and a mutual reverence for the partner's life and personhood. Francis and Jane show us that mutuality, beginning with their core relationship, then extends out to other friendships and beyond these bonds to the community at large. It does so because mutuality reflects the relationship between the human person and God. It is covenantal. It is the presence of God's grace that makes any relationship sacramental, whether with our spouse, our best friend, our children, or our neighbors.

Francis and Jane, and all the saints in this book, show us that our relationship with God is fully mutual. God gives himself to us; we give ourselves to God. We are in relationship. And – good news – the gift of mutuality is something that can be developed through awareness, solitude, fellowship, charity, and prayer.

As Martin Luther said, "We are not now what we shall be, but we are on the way." Spiritual growth is a lifelong process, rooted in the deepening of love, wisdom, and understanding.

Perfection of life is the perfection of love.
For love is the life of the soul.

—FRANCIS DE SALES

Acknowledgments

During the writing of this book, I received the miraculous gift of time, and I wish to thank my husband, Michael, and my children, Emma and Hanna, for granting me that so generously.

I also wish to thank the Department of Theology and the Graduate School of Religious Education at Fordham University; Professor John J. Shea of Boston College; the Maryknoll Fathers and Sisters; the parish of St. Ignatius Loyola in New York City; Fr. Damian O'Connell; the Franciscan Friars and Sisters of the Atonement at Graymoor, New York; the Convent of St. Helena at Vails Gate, New York; Rev. Dr. D. Elizabeth Mauro and the Rockland Congregational Church in Rockland, Maine; the Maine Media Women; and the Camden Deli in Camden, Maine, where I made revisions accompanied by many an iced latté.

Finally, I wish to thank my editorial consultant, Roy M. Carlisle, my publisher, Gwendolin Herder, and all the staff at The Crossroad Publishing Company for their personal and professional support.

Permissions

"Before I Could Discern Many Profiles 2" / "The Crypt" / "Words Spoken by the Woman at the Well on Departing" from THE PLACE WITHIN by Karol Wojtyla, translated by Jerzy Peterkiewics, published by Hutchinson. Reprinted by permission of The Random House Group Ltd.

Image of Francis de Sales and Jane de Chantal by Mary Ford. Copyright DeSales Spirituality Center. Used with permission. www.oblates.org/spirituality

Image of Catherine of Sienna. The work of art depicted in this image and the reproduction thereof are in the public domain worldwide. The reproduction is part of a collection of reproductions compiled by The Yorck Project. The compilation copyright is held by The Yorck Project and licensed under the GNU Free Documentation License.

Quote from "Moonstruck" used with permission of John Patrick Shanley.

Bibliography
& Other Sources

Barnstone, Willis, trans. *The Poems of Saint John of the Cross.* 1968. Bloomington: Indiana University Press.

Bielecki, Tessa. *Teresa of Avila: Mystical Writings.* 1994. New York: Crossroad.

Bodo, Murray. *Clare: A Light in the Garden.* 1992. Cincinatti: St. Anthony Messenger Press.

Brady, Ignatius. *The Prayers of Saint Francis.* 1988. Ann Arbor: Servant Books.

Cuthbert, OSFC, Fr. *The Little Flowers of St. Francis of Assisi.* 1912. London: Catholic Truth Society.

De Robeck, Nesta. *St. Clare of Assisi.* 1980. Chicago: Franciscan Herald Press.

Dicken, E. W. Trueman. *The Crucible of Love: A Study of the Mysticism of St. Teresa of Jesus and St. John of the Cross.* 1963. New York: Sheed and Ward.

Endean, Philip, and Editors. "Contemporary Reflections on the Spirituality of Clare. The Way" *Supplement* 80. London: 1994.

Farina, John, et al. *Francis de Sales and Jane de Chantal: Letters of Spiritual Direction.* The Classics of Western Spirituality. 1988. New York: Paulist Press.

Frances, Teresa, OSC, Sr. *This Living Mirror: Reflections on Clare of Assisi.* 1995. Maryknoll: Orbis.

Gasnick, Roy M. *The Francis Book.* 1980. New York: MacMillan.

Hallundbaek, Carole. *Dear Little One: Thoughts to My Child in an Uncertain World.* 2005. New York: Crossroad.

Hamilton, Edith. *Mythology: Timeless Tales of Gods and Heroes.* 1940, 1942, 1969. New York: NAL Penguin Inc.

Kavanaugh, Kieran, OCD. *The Collected Letters of St. Teresa of Avila.* 2001. Washington, D.C.: ICS Publications, Institute of Carmelite Studies.

Kavanaugh, Kieran, and Otilio Rodriguez. *The Collected Works of St. Teresa of Avila.* 3 vols. 1976, 1980, 1985. Washington, D.C.: ICS Publications.

Lewis, C. S. *The Four Loves.* 1960, 1988. New York: Harcourt Brace & Company.

Meade, Catherine M., CSJ. *My Nature Is Fire: Saint Catherine of Siena.* 1991. New York: Alba House.

Morris, Gunilla. *Becoming Bread.* 1993. New York: Bell Tower.

Noffke, Suzanne and Guiliana Cavallini, Editors in Chief. Catherine of Siena: *The Dialogue* 1980. The Classics of Western Spirituality New York: Paulist Press.

Payne, Richard J., Editor in Chief. *Francis and Clare: The Complete Works.* 1982. The Classics of Western Spirituality. New York: Paulist Press.

Payne, Richard J., et al. *Teresa of Avila: The Interior Castle.* 1979. The Classics of Western Spirituality. New York: Paulist Press.

Shea, John J. *Finding God Again: Spirituality for Adults.* 2005. Lanham: Rowman & Littlefield Publishers, Inc.

Unknown. *The Little Flowers of St. Francis of Assisi* (The *Fioretti*). 1912. London: Catholic Truth Society.

Wojtyla, Karol. *Easter Vigil & Other Poems.* 1979. New York: Random House.

Wojtyla, Karol. *The Place Within: The Poetry of Pope John Paul II.* Translated by Jerzy Peterkiewics. 1995. London: Hutchinson.

About the Author

CAROLE HALLUNDBAEK is an award-winning author, coun-selor, spiritual director and consultant. She is an on-air host and  commentator on religion and spirituality for national news media, and has hosted the TV program on faith, 'Winds of Change.' Carole received her graduate degrees in theology and religion from Maryknoll School of Theology and Fordham University. Co-founder of The Godspeed Institute, she lives in coastal Maine with her family. To learn more, visit www.carolehallundbaek.com.

Of Related Interest

Pope John Paul II
Edited by Carl J. Moell, S.J.
HOLY FATHER, SACRED HEART
The Complete Collection of John Paul II's Writings
on the Perennial Catholic Devotion

Pope John Paul II has given the devotion to the Sacred Heart a special place in his spiritual life and public ministry for decades. In *Holy Father, Sacred Heart,* Carl J. Moell, drawing from his experience working with the Society of Jesus in Rome, gathers together every teaching the Holy Father has proclaimed regarding this most intimate of Catholic devotions. From the Pope's speeches before audiences of millions, to his personal prayers and writings, *Holy Father, Sacred Heart* is the perfect treasury for everyone devoted to the Sacred Heart of Jesus Christ.

0-8245-2147-1, paperback

crossroad

Of Related Interest

Carole Hallundbaek
DEAR LITTLE ONE
Thoughts to My Child in an Uncertain World

Assembled as a precious gift book, these profound and loving reflections of hope and wisdom draw us into the special intimacy of the parent-child relationship. Reflections include: New Life, You Are Never Alone, Marriage, Humility, and many others.

0-8245-2312-1, hardcover

Madonna Sophia Compton
with Maria Compton Hernandez and Patricia Campbell
WOMEN SAINTS
365 Daily Readings

The most inspiring book of its kind ever written. In this perfect gift volume, Madonna Sophia Compton offers us 365 daily readings from women saints of all the major Christian traditions, with special attention to the Marian feast days. Each day features a meditation on a holy woman celebrated on that day, followed by an original prayer and a scripture reading.

0-8245-2413-6, paperback

crossroad

Of Related Interest

Tolbert McCarroll
A WINTER WALK

Few storytellers can capture the sense of the divine as Brother Toby can. In this precious gift book we are invited to stroll along with this outstanding monk through the wintry season of darkness, candlelight, and the rich symbols and celebrations of all faiths. Each reflection enhances our appreciation of its topic, including the Advent Wreath, Bodhi Day, Chanukah, Ramadan, Santa Lucia, and Epiphany.

"We have all experienced times and places where we encountered something transcendent. Ancient Celtic peoples referred to these experiences as 'thin places' where two parallel worlds come together. . . . If we are mindful, we can find 'thin places' in those walls where we discover there doesn't have to be much difference between the sacred and the ordinary. In the cycle of the seasons, winter is the 'thin place.' "
— *From the book*

Tolbert McCarroll, "Brother Toby," is a monk, spiritual director, and author of eight books, including *Notes from the Song of Life, Exploring the Inner World, Monksong,* and *Thinking with the Heart.* He is a monk at Starcross, a small lay community in the monastic tradition, based in Sonoma County, California.

0-8245-2416-0, hardcover

crossroad

Of Related Interest

Paula D'Arcy
SACRED THRESHOLD
Crossing the Inner Barrier to Deeper Love

In the midst of her own story of recovery from devastating life events, we journey with Paula D'Arcy as she seeks to counsel clients and relate to friends and family when conventional ways of relating are not good enough. The book features the story Paula's work with Morrie Schwartz of *Tuesdays with Morrie* as well as the stories of her journey with Julia, a woman serving a prison sentence for drunk driving; Scott, a troubled young boy; and with her aging father. These powerful stories invite us to reconsider the nature of love and the thresholds we must cross in order to love honestly.

"Paula captures with clarity the mysterious desire of our hearts — to love outside the walls of convention, and experience love's miraculous transformation. A must read."

— Carmen Renee Berry, co-author of
New York Times bestseller *girlfriends*

0-8245-2465-9, paperback

crossroad

Of Related Interest

Robert Ellsberg
BLESSED AMONG ALL WOMEN
Women Saints, Prophets, and Witnesses for Our Time

With a record-tying three Catholic Press Awards to its name, *Blessed Among All Women* has been a sensation in religious publishing. Robert Ellsberg gained renown with his first book, *All Saints,* which has become a modern classic of devotional literature. Using that classic as his starting point, Ellsberg's *Blessed Among All Women* offers devotional sketches on history's greatest women. The material is organized around the Beatitudes, with each section discussing women who have excelled in one aspect of spiritual life — including peacemaking and purity of heart.

0-8245-2439-X, paperback

crossroad

Of Related Interest

Peter M. Kalellis, Ph.D.
RESTORING RELATIONSHIPS
Five Things to Try Before You Say Goodbye

This fascinating book promises to restore broken or fragmented relationships. It offers concrete ways to put five important principles into practice so that any relationship may grow and regain peace and productivity.

0-8245-1880-2, paperback

Check your local bookstore for availability.
To order directly from the publisher,
please call 1-800-707-0670 for Customer Service
or visit our Web site at *www.cpcbooks.com.*
For catalog orders, please send your request to the address below.

THE CROSSROAD PUBLISHING COMPANY
16 Penn Plaza, Suite 1550
New York, NY 10001

crossroad